IMPORTANT INSTR...

Use the URL or QR code provided below to unlock all the online learning resources included with this Grade 7 to 8 summer learning activities workbook.

URL	QR CODE
Visit the URL below for online registration **www.lumoslearning.com/a/sg7-8** **Access Code: SLHG7-8ML-17562-S**	

 YOUR ONLINE ACCESS INCLUDES

- ✓ Skills practice resources for Grade 8 Math and ELA.
- ✓ Grade-appropriate passages to improve reading skills.
- ✓ Grade 7 vocabulary quizzes.
- ✓ Access to Lumos Flashcube - An interactive tool to improve vocabulary.
- ✓ Educational videos, worksheets, standards information and more.

 ADDITIONAL BENEFITS OF ONLINE REGISTRATION

- ✓ Entry to Lumos Weekly Summer Photo Contest
- ✓ Entry to Lumos Short Story Competition

Lumos Learning
Step Up Your Skills

Lumos Summer Learning HeadStart, Grade 7 to 8, Student Copy: Fun Activities, Math, Reading, Vocabulary, Writing and Language Practice

Contributing Author	- Stacy Zeiger
Contributing Author	- Aaron Spencer
Contributing Author	- Julie C. Lyons
Contributing Editor	- George Smith
Contributing Editor	- Marisa Adams
Executive Producer	- Mukunda Krishnaswamy
Database Administrator	- R. Raghavendra Rao
Designer and Illustrator	- Snehal Sharan

ISBN 13: 9781097422555

Printed in the United States of America

Last Updated: March 2023

FOR SCHOOL EDITION AND PERMISSIONS, CONTACT US

LUMOS INFORMATION SERVICES, LLC

 PO Box 1575, Piscataway, NJ 08855-1575
 www.LumosLearning.com

✉ Email: support@lumoslearning.com
☎ Tel: (732) 384-0146
📠 Fax: (866) 283-6471

Lumos Learning
Step Up Your Skills

TABLE OF CONTENTS

🌐 **Online Activity** | Daily Challenge | Reading Assignment | Vocabulary Practice | Summer Diary |

🌐 **Online Activity** | Daily Challenge | Reading Assignment | Vocabulary Practice | Summer Diary |

🌐 **Online Activity** | Daily Challenge | Reading Assignment | Vocabulary Practice | Summer Diary

Lumos Learning
Step Up Your Skills

FUN & ENGAGING

ONLINE SUMMER PRACTICE

GET DIGITAL ACCESS TO

 Daily Challenge Round (Math & ELA)

 Weekly Fun Activities

 Reading & Vocabulary Exercises

 Summer Diary

 Preview to Grade 8 Math & ELA

REGISTER NOW

Access Code: SLHG7-8ML-17562-S

www.lumoslearning.com/a/sg7-8

INTRODUCTION

Summer break is an exciting time for children as it brings an opportunity to enjoy the outdoors, relax, and explore new activities. However, it also presents the challenge of summer academic learning loss. Let's understand what summer academic learning loss is and how you can use this book to effectively combat it.

What is Summer Academic Learning Loss?

This phenomenon is the loss of knowledge and skills that students experience during the summer break, which can cause a drop in their standardized testing scores when they return to school. As a result, teachers often spend the first four to five weeks of the school year re-teaching critical material that students have forgotten.

In subjects like math, students lose an average of two-and-a-half months of skills during the summer break. When reading and math losses are combined, the average loss is three months, and it may be even greater for some students. The three areas where students typically experience the most significant decline are spelling, vocabulary, and mathematics.

How to Use This Workbook Effectively During Summer

Encourage your child to engage in academic activities every day, such as reading, writing, or doing math problems. The activities in this book are organized by week and aligned with the current grade-level learning standards. We encourage you to start at the beginning of summer holidays. During each week, students can complete the daily Math and English practice. There are five daily practice worksheets for each week.

Further, the online program also provides daily challenges in Math and English and weekly activities in reading, vocabulary and writing. Students can also explore fun activities included in the program anytime during the week. Additionally, students can record their Summer activity through the online program.

The online program also includes a limited access to next-grade learning resources. This section of the online program could be used to help students to get a glimpse of what they would be learning in the next grade level.

By implementing this short and effective daily practice routine, educators and parents can help keep their children academically engaged during the summer months and prevent the detrimental effects of summer learning loss.

1. A tennis match was delayed because of rain. The officials were not prepared for the delay. They covered the 25ft by 20ft court with 13ft by 10ft plastic covers. How many plastic covers were needed to cover the court from the rain?

   Ⓐ 3 plastic covers
   Ⓑ 4 plastic covers
   Ⓒ 5 plastic covers
   Ⓓ 6 plastic covers

2. John eats a bowl of cereal for 3 of his 4 meals each day. He finishes two gallons of milk in eight days. How much milk does John use for one bowl of cereal? (Assume he only uses the milk for his cereal.)

   Ⓐ One-twelfth of a gallon of milk
   Ⓑ One cup of milk
   Ⓒ Two cups of milk
   Ⓓ One-sixth of a gallon of milk

3. A recipe to make a cake calls for three-fourths of a cup of milk. Mary used this cake as the first layer of a wedding cake. The second layer was half the size of the first layer, and the third layer was half the size of the second layer. How much milk would be used for the entire wedding cake?

   Ⓐ one and two-thirds cups of milk
   Ⓑ one and one-third cups of milk
   Ⓒ one and five-sixteenths cups of milk
   Ⓓ one cup of milk

4. What is the unit rate for a pound of seed? Circle the correct answer choice.

Pounds of Seed	Total Cost
10	$17.50
20	$35.00
30	$52.50
40	$70.00

   Ⓐ $3.50
   Ⓑ $1.75
   Ⓒ $17.50
   Ⓓ $7.25

From *Scouting for Boys*

Read the story below and answer the questions that follow.

"Hi! Stop Thief!" shouted old Blenkinsopp as he rushed out of his little store near the village.
"He's stolen my sugar. Stop him."

Stop whom? There was nobody in sight running away, "Who stole it?" asked the policeman.

"I don't know, but a whole bag of sugar is missing. It was there only a few minutes ago." The policeman tried to track the thief, but it looked a pretty impossible job for him to single out the tracks of the thief from among dozens of other footprints about the store. However, he presently started off hopefully, at a jog-trot, away out into the bush. In some places, he went over the hard stony ground, but he never checked his pace, although no footmarks could be seen. People wondered how he could possibly find the trail. Still, he trotted on. Old Blenkinsopp was feeling the heat and the pace.

At length, he suddenly stopped and cast around, having evidently lost the trail. Then a grin came on his face as he pointed with his thumb over his shoulder up the tree near which he was standing. There, concealed among the branches, they saw a young man with the missing bag of sugar.

How had the policeman spotted him? His sharp eyes had detected some grains of sugar sparkling in the dust. The bag leaked, leaving a slight trail of these grains. He followed that trail, and when it came to an end in the bush, he noticed a string of ants going up a tree. They were after the sugar, and so was he, and between them, they brought about the capture of the thief.

Old Blenkinsopp was so pleased that he promptly opened the bag and spilled a lot of the sugar on the ground as a reward to the ants.

He also appreciated the policeman for his cleverness in using his eyes to see the grains of sugar and the ants, and in using his wits to know why the ants were climbing the tree.

5. Why could the policeman not find the footprints from among the others in the shop?

Ⓐ because they were clearly marked
Ⓑ there were dozens of footprints
Ⓒ there were no footprints to be found
Ⓓ the footprints had been cleaned

Read the story below and answer the questions that follow.

For years, Sam had dreamed of being the best tennis player in the world. He went to tennis practice every single morning and night. He spent every summer at tennis camp, and he gave up long weekends at the beach to work on his game. Now, it seemed his hard work was finally paying off: He was invited to try out for the state tennis team!

Still, there was something that was bothering Sam. The tryouts for the tennis team were on the same day as his mom's birthday, and he knew his family was planning a huge surprise party for her. He didn't want to hurt his mom's feelings by missing the party, but he also didn't want to miss his one shot at being a champion tennis player. He was in a quandary; he didn't know what to do.

For days, Sam went to bed, worrying about the decision. If he went to the tryout, he worried he would seem selfish. If he stayed home, he would miss his one big shot at making the state team. In fact, despite the honor of being invited to try out, he hadn't even told his family about the opportunity. He was so stressed about making the decision of whether to go or not that he couldn't even think about sharing the news.

Weeks went by, and Sam was making no progress. Every day his coach asked him if he was ready for the tryout, and Sam couldn't even respond. Finally, Sam couldn't bear the stress any longer. He decided to talk to his grandfather about his predicament.

"You know, your mom wants you to be happy," he told Sam. "It would be a great birthday present for her to know you are making your dream come true."

Sam had never thought of it that way before, and after talking to his grandfather, he knew what he had to do. He immediately went home and sat down with his parents to let them know about the opportunity to try out for the state team. When Sam apologetically told his parents what day the tryouts were, they were so busy shrieking with excitement that he thought maybe they hadn't heard.

"But Mom, that means I'm going to miss your birthday," Sam said. "I am happy you are so nice about it, but I still feel really bad."

"Are you kidding?" his mom asked. "This is the best present I could ask for!"

6. In this passage, who helps Sam make his choice?

Ⓐ His dog
Ⓑ His neighbor
Ⓒ His grandfather
Ⓓ His mom

7. Which of the following is NOT a sign that Sam's parents raised him well?

Ⓐ He understood that family and tennis were both priorities he needed to balance in his life.
Ⓑ He sought guidance from his grandfather instead of running from the problem.
Ⓒ He knew that to become a great tennis player he had to put in a lot of hard work.
Ⓓ Sam didn't care about missing the party.

Lines Written In A Young Lady's Album
By George W. Sands

Read the poem below and answer the questions that follow.

'Tis not in youth, when life is new, when but to live is sweet,
When Pleasure strews her starlikeflow'rs beneath our careless feet,
When Hope, that has not been deferred, first waves its golden wings,
And crowds the distant future with a thousand lovely things; -

When if a transient grief o'ershades the spirit for a while,
The momentary tear that falls is followed by a smile;
Or if a pensive mood, at times, across the bosom steals,
It scarcely sighs, so gentle is the pensiveness it feels

It is not then the, restless soul will seek for one with whom
To share whatever lot it bears, its gladness or its gloom, -
Some trusting, tried, and gentle heart, some true and faithful breast,
Whereon its pinions it may fold, and claim a place of rest.

But oh! when comes the icy chill that freezes o'er the heart,
When, one by one, the joys we shared, the hopes we held, depart;
When friends, like autumn's withered leaves, have fallen by our side,
And life, so pleasant once, becomes a desert wild and wide; -

As for her olive branch the dove swept o'er the sullen wave,
That rolled above the olden world - its death-robe and its grave! -
So will the spirit search the earth for some kind, gentle one,
With it to share her destiny, and make it all her own!

8. **What do you think the poet is writing about in this poem? Write your answer in the box below.**

1. The following table shows two variables in a proportional relationship:

a	b
2	6
3	9
4	12

Which of the following is an algebraic statement showing the relationship between a and b.

- Ⓐ a = 3b
- Ⓑ b = 3a
- Ⓒ b = 1/3 (a)
- Ⓓ a = 1/2 (b)

2. If the ratio of the length of a rectangle to its width is 3 to 2, what is the length of a rectangle whose width is 4 inches?

- Ⓐ 4 in.
- Ⓑ 5 in.
- Ⓒ 6 in.
- Ⓓ 7 in.

3. The following table shows two variables in a proportional relationship:

e	f
5	25
6	30
7	35

Using the relationship between e and f as shown in this table, find the value of f when e = 11.

- Ⓐ 40
- Ⓑ 45
- Ⓒ 50
- Ⓓ 55

4. The table shows a proportional relationship between x and y. For each value of x and y, match it to the correct unit rate $\dfrac{y}{x}$ in it's simplest form.

	$\dfrac{6}{1}$	$\dfrac{3}{1}$	$\dfrac{9}{1}$
x = 3 and y = 27			
x = 9 and y = 81			
x = 21 and y = 126			
x = 14 and y = 84			
x = 12 and y = 36			
x = 15 and y = 45			

"The Lament" by Sravani

Read the story below and answer the questions that follow.

It is twilight. Thick wet snow is slowly twirling around the newly lighted street lamps and lying in soft thin layers on roofs, on horses' backs, on people's shoulders and hats. The cab driver, Iona Potapov, is quite white and looks like a phantom: he is bent double as far as a human body can bend double; he is seated on his box; he never makes a move. If a whole snowdrift fell on him, it seems as if he would not find it necessary to shake it off. His little horse is also quite white, and remains motionless; its immobility, its angularity, and its straight wooden-looking legs, even close by, give it the appearance of a gingerbread horse worth a kopek. It is, no doubt, plunged in deep thought. If you were snatched from the plough, from your usual gray surroundings, and were thrown into this slough full of monstrous lights, unceasing noise and hurrying people, you too would find it difficult not to think.

Iona and his little horse have not moved from their place for a long while. They left their yard before dinner and, up to now, not a fare. The evening mist is descending over the town, the white lights of the lamps are replacing brighter rays, and the hubbub of the street is getting louder.

'Cabby for Viborg Way!' suddenly hears Iona. 'Cabby!'
Iona jumps and, through his snow-covered eyelashes, sees an officer in a greatcoat, with his hood
over his head.

'Viborg way!' the officer repeats. 'Are you asleep, eh? Viborg way!'
With a nod of assent, Iona picks up the reins, in consequence of which layers of snow slip off the horse's back and neck. The officer seats himself in the sleigh, the cab driver smacks his lips to encourage his horse, stretches out his neck like a swan, sits up and, more from habit than necessity, brandishes his whip. The little horse also stretches its neck, bends its wooden-looking legs, and makes a move undecidedly.

'What are you doing, werewolf!' is the exclamation Iona hears from the dark mass moving to and fro, as soon as they have started.
'Where the devil are you going? To the r-r-right!'
'You do not know how to drive. Keep to the right!' calls the officer angrily. A coachman from a private carriage swears at him; a passerby, who has run across the road and rubbed his shoulder against the horse's nose, looks at him furiously as he sweeps the snow from his sleeve. Iona shifts about on his seat as if he was on needles, moves his elbows as if he were trying to keep his equilibrium, and gasps about like someone suffocating, who does not understand why and wherefore he is there.

'What scoundrels they all are!' jokes the officer; 'one would think they had all entered into an agreement to jostle you or fall under your horse.'
Iona looks around at the officer and moves his lips. He evidently wants to say something but the only sound that issues is a snuffle.
'What?' asks the officer.
Iona twists his mouth into a smile and, with an effort, says hoarsely:
'My son, Barin, died this week.'
'Hm! What did he die of?'
Iona turns with his whole body towards his fare and says: 'And who knows! They say high

fever. He was three days in the hospital and then died... God's will be done.'

"Turn round! The devil!' sounds from the darkness. 'Have you popped off, old doggie, eh? Use your eyes!'

'Go on, go on,' says the officer, 'otherwise we shall not get there by tomorrow. Hurry up a bit!'

"If you were snatched from the plough, from your usual gray surroundings, and were thrown into this slough full of monstrous lights, unceasing noise and hurrying people, you too would find it difficult not to think."

5. **What can be inferred from the first two paragraphs of the passage?**

   Ⓐ that the cab driver was very sad
   Ⓑ that the cabby was from a village or a very small town
   Ⓒ that the cab driver did not want to think
   Ⓓ that the cab driver was not thinking

"Bruno the Bear"
Excerpt from *The Bond of Love*

Read the story below and answer the questions that follow.

I will begin with Bruno, my wife's pet sloth bear. I got him for her by accident. Two years ago, we were passing through the cornfields near a small town in Iowa. People were driving away the wild pigs from the fields by shooting at them. Some were shot, and some escaped. We thought that everything was over when suddenly a black sloth bear came out panting in the hot sun.

Now I will not shoot a sloth bear wantedly, but unfortunately for the poor beast, one of my companions did not feel the same way about it and promptly shot the bear on the spot.

As we watched the fallen animal, we were surprised to see that the black fur on its back moved and left the prostrate body. Then we saw it was a baby bear that had been riding on its mother's back when the sudden shot had killed her. The little creature ran around its prostrate parent, making a pitiful noise. I ran up to it to attempt a capture. It scooted into the sugarcane field. Following it with my companions, I was at last able to grab it by the scruff of its neck while it snapped and tried to scratch me with its long, hooked claws.

We put it in one of the large jute-bags we had brought, and when I got back home, I duly presented it to my wife. She was delighted! She at once put a blue colored ribbon around its neck, and after discovering the cub was a 'boy,' she christened it Bruno.

Bruno soon took to drinking milk from a bottle. It was but a step further, and within a very few days, he started eating and drinking everything else. And everything is the right word, for he ate porridge made from any ingredients, vegetables, fruit, nuts, meat (especially pork), curry and rice regardless of condiments and chilies, bread, eggs, chocolates, sweets, pudding, ice-cream, etc. As for drink: milk, tea, coffee, lime juice, aerated water, buttermilk, beer, alcoholic liquor, and, in fact, anything liquid. It all went down with relish.

The bear became very attached to our two dogs and all the children living in and around our farm. He was left quite free in his younger days and spent his time playing, running into the kitchen, and going to sleep in our beds.

One day an accident befell him. I put down poison (barium carbonate) to kill the rats and mice that had got into my library. Bruno entered the library as he often did and ate some of the poison. Paralysis set into the extent that he could not stand on his feet. But he dragged himself on his stumps to my wife, who called me. I guessed what had happened.

Off I rushed him in the car to the vet's residence. A case of poisoning! Tame Bear—barium carbonate— what to do? Out came his medical books, and a feverish reference to index began: "What poison did you say, sir?" he asked, "Barium carbonate," I said.

"Ah yes—B—Ba—Barium Salts—Ah! Barium carbonate! Symptoms— paralysis—treatment—injections of . .. Just a minute, sir. I'll bring my syringe and the medicine." Said the doc. I dashed back to the car. Bruno was still floundering about on his stumps, but clearly, he was weakening rapidly; there was some vomiting, he was breathing heavily, with heaving flanks and gaping mouth. I was really scared and did not know what to do. I was feeling very guilty and was running in and out of the vet's house doing everything the doc asked me.

"Hold him, everybody!" In goes the hypodermic—Bruno squeals — 10 c.c. of the antidote enters his system without a drop being wasted. Ten minutes later: condition unchanged! Another 10 c.c. Injected! Ten minutes later: breathing less torturous— Bruno can move his arms and legs a little although he cannot stand yet. Thirty minutes later: Bruno gets up and has a great feed! He looks at us disdainfully, as much as to say, 'What's barium carbonate to a big black bear like me?' Bruno was still eating. I was really happy to see him recover.

The months rolled on, and Bruno had grown many times the size he was when he came. He had equaled the big dogs in height and had even outgrown them. But was just as sweet, just as mischievous, just as playful. And he was very fond of us all. Above all, he loved my wife, and she loved him too! And he could do a few tricks, too. At the command, 'Bruno, wrestle,' or 'Bruno, box,' he vigorously tackled anyone who came forward for a rough and tumble. Give him a stick and say 'Bruno, hold the gun,' and he pointed the stick at you. Ask him, 'Bruno, where's baby?' and he immediately produced and cradled affectionately a stump of wood which he had carefully concealed in his straw bed. But because of the neighborhoods' and our renters' children, poor Bruno, had to be kept chained most of the time.

Then my son and I advised my wife and friends advised her, too, to give Bruno to the zoo. He was getting too big to keep at home. After some weeks of such advice, she at last consented. Hastily, and before she could change her mind, a letter was written to the curator of the zoo. Did he want a tame bear for his collection? He replied, "Yes." The zoo sent a cage in a truck, a distance of hundred – eighty – seven miles, and Bruno was packed off. We all missed him greatly, but in a sense, we were relieved. My wife was inconsolable. She wept and fretted. For the first few days, she would not eat a thing. Then she wrote a number of letters to the curator. How was Bruno? Back came the replies, "Well, but fretting; he refuses food too."

After that, friends visiting the zoo were begged to make a point of seeing how Bruno was getting along. They reported that he was well but looked very thin and sad. All the keepers at the zoo said he was fretting. For three months, I managed to restrain my wife from visiting the zoo. Then she said one day, "I must see Bruno. Either you take me by car, or I will go myself by bus or train myself." So I took her by car. Friends had conjectured that the bear would not recognize her. I had thought so too. But while she was yet some yards from his cage, Bruno saw her and recognized her. He howled with happiness. She ran up to him, petted him through the bars, and he stood on his head in delight.

For the next three hours, she would not leave that cage. She gave him tea, lemonade, cakes, ice cream, and whatnot. Then 'closing time' came and we had to leave. My wife cried bitterly; Bruno cried bitterly; even the hardened curator and the keepers felt depressed. As for me, I had reconciled myself to what I knew was going to happen next.

"Oh please, sir," she asked the curator, "may I have my Bruno back"? Hesitantly, he answered, "Madam, he belongs to the zoo and is Government property now. I cannot give away Government property. But if my boss, the superintendent, agrees, certainly, you may have him back."

There followed the return journey home and a visit to the superintendent's office. A tearful pleading: "Bruno and I are both fretting for each other. Will you please give him back to me?" He was a kind-hearted man and consented. Not only that, but he wrote to the curator, telling him to lend us a cage for transporting the bear back home.

Back we went to the zoo again, armed with the superintendent's letter. Bruno was driven into a small cage and hoisted on top of the car; the cage was tied securely, and a slow and careful return journey back home was accomplished.

Once home, a squad of workers were engaged for special work around our yard. An island was made for Bruno. It was twenty feet long and fifteen feet wide and was surrounded by a dry moat, six feet wide and seven feet deep. A wooden box that once housed fowls was brought and put on the island for Bruno to sleep in at night. Straw was placed inside to keep him warm, and his 'baby,' the gnarled stump, along with his 'gun,' the piece of bamboo, both of which had been sentimentally preserved since he had been sent away to the zoo, were put back for him to play with. In a few days, the workers hoisted the cage on to the island, and Bruno was released. He was delighted; standing on his hind legs, he pointed his 'gun' and cradled his 'baby.' My wife spent hours sitting on a chair there while he sat on her lap. He was fifteen months old and pretty heavy too!

The way my wife reaches the island and leaves it is interesting. I have tied a rope to the overhanging branch of a maple tree with a loop at its end. Putting one foot in the loop, she kicks off with the other, to bridge the six-foot gap that constitutes the width of the surrounding moat. The return journey back is made the same way.

But who can say now that a sloth bear has no sense of affection, no memory, and no individual characteristics?

6. How can the reader infer the bear was depressed?

    Ⓐ because both the bear and the author's wife cried bitterly while departing
    Ⓑ because the bear did not recognize its mistress
    Ⓒ because the author's wife was lean and depressed
    Ⓓ because Bruno would not eat anything.

Read the story below and answer the questions that follow.

Ever since they were kids, Julie and Max had been best friends. They went to kindergarten together. They went to summer camp together; They hung out together every weekend. But suddenly, things between the two had started to change.

Max had started playing on the football team and didn't have much time for Julie anymore. He was always busy, and he never seemed to make it to study hall, where the two used to swap stories about their favorite (or least favorite) teachers. In class, Julie noticed that Max never seemed to have his homework done on time anymore. She even noticed that he got a D on his last paper. She knew something was going on with him – but what?

At first, Julie decided to play it cool and see how things went. She tried waiting in the hall for Max after class to see if she could ask if he was OK. But days went by, and he never had time to stop.He'd rush right past her in the hall, only to leave her feeling even worse about what was happening between them.

Even though she wasn't sure she could handle the situation herself, Julie didn't want to talk to her parents because she was afraid they would tell her not to hang out with Max any-more. She barely saw him as it was, so she knew it would just make things worse if her parents didn't approve of him. She didn't want to tell Max's parents either because she didn't want him to get in trouble. Still, it seemed like something needed to change. Julie decided to go to one of her school counselors and let her

know she was concerned.

When she walked into Mrs. Smith's room, she was surprised to see that Max was already sitting there.
"I'm sorry, I'll come back," Julie said.
"No, stay," said Max. "Maybe you can help."

Julie was surprised to find that Max had visited the counselor's office for the same reason she had: He was starting to feel overwhelmed with all of the things he was supposed to be doing as a student, an athlete, and a friend. He needed some guidance on how to determine what truly mattered and how to divide his time between all of the things that were important to him. When she realized that Max was still the same old Max (just a little more stressed), Julie was relieved. She was also happy to know that he had come to a conclusion on his own, without her having to talk to someone else about it. She decided it was a sign they were both growing up.

7. What can you infer about relationship between Julie and Max?

Ⓐ They were best of friends who cared about each other.
Ⓑ They really hated each other, so they went to the counselor alone.
Ⓒ They were just acquaintances who only occasionally talked.
Ⓓ They were neighbors.

Read the story below and answer the questions that follow.

For years, Sam had dreamed of being the best tennis player in the world. He went to tennis practice every single morning and every single night. He spent every summer at tennis camp, and he gave up long weekends at the beach to work on his game. Now, it seemed his hard work was finally paying off: he was invited to try out for the state tennis team!

Still, there was something that was bothering Sam. The tryouts for the tennis team were on the same day as his mom's birthday, and he knew his family was planning a huge surprise party for her. He didn't want to hurt his mom's feelings by missing the party, but he also didn't want to miss his one shot at being a champion tennis player just because the tryouts were on his mom's birthday. He was in a quandary; he didn't know what to do.

For days, Sam went to bed worrying about the decision. If he went to the tryout, he worried he would seem selfish. If he stayed home, he would miss his one big shot at making the state team. In fact, despite the honor of being invited to try out, he hadn't even told his family about the opportunity. He was so stressed about making the decision of whether to go that he couldn't even think about sharing the news.

Weeks went by, and Sam was making no progress. Every day his coach asked him if he was ready for the tryout, and Sam couldn't even respond. Finally, Sam couldn't bear the stress any longer. He decided to talk to his grandfather about his predicament.

"You know, your mom wants you to be happy," he told Sam. "It would be a great birthday present for her to know you are making your dream come true."

Sam had never thought of it that way before, and after talking to his grandfather, he knew what he had to do. He immediately went home and sat down with his parents to let them know about the opportunity to try out for the state team. His parents were so excited that when he told them, apologetically, what day the tryouts were, and they were so busy shrieking with excitement that he thought maybe they hadn't heard.

"But Mom, that means I'm going to miss your birthday," Sam said. "I am happy you are being so nice about it, but I still feel really bad."

"Are you kidding?" his mom asked? "This is the best present I could ask for!"

8. Which of the following is a sign that Sam's parents raised him well?

Ⓐ He understood that family and tennis were both priorities he needed to balance in his life
Ⓑ He sought guidance from his grandfather instead of running from the problem
Ⓒ He knew that to become a great tennis player he had to put in a lot of hard work
Ⓓ All of the above

DAY 2

CHALLENGE YOURSELF!
✔ Understanding and Representing Proportions
✔ Use Those Clues – Make an Inference

🌐 www.lumoslearning.com/a/dc7-2

See the first page for Signup details

1. According to the graph, what is the constant of proportionality?

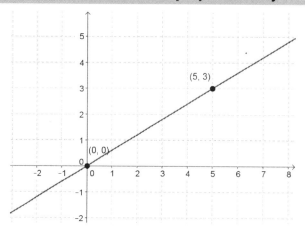

Ⓐ $\dfrac{3}{5}$

Ⓑ 5

Ⓒ 3

Ⓓ $\dfrac{1}{3}$

2. According to the table, how much does one ticket cost?

Number of Tickets	Total Cost
3	$ 21.00
4	$ 28.00
5	$ 35.00
6	$ 42.00

Ⓐ $21.00
Ⓑ $4.75
Ⓒ $7.00
Ⓓ $16.50

3. If y = 3x, what is the constant of proportionality between y and x?

    Ⓐ 1
    Ⓑ 0.30
    Ⓒ 1.50
    Ⓓ 3

4. In proportional relationships, there are dependent and independent variables. Match each situation to whether it is an independent variable or not.

	Independent Variable	Dependent Variable
The number of concert tickets sold is based on how many hours the ticket booth is open. What kind of variable is the number of hours the ticket booth is open?		
The number of cans that is collected for a charity drive is based on how many students bring in cans. What kind of variable is the number of students?		
The number of buses needed for a field trip depends on how many students are going on the field trip. What kind of variable is the number of buses?		
The number of cell phone towers built is determined by how many customers are in the area. What kind of variable is the number of cell phone towers?		

"Bruno the Bear"
Excerpt from *The Bond of Love*

Read the story below and answer the questions that follow.

I will begin with Bruno, my wife's pet sloth bear. I got him for her by accident. Two years ago, we were passing through the cornfields near a small town in Iowa. People were driving away the wild pigs from the fields by shooting at them. Some were shot, and some escaped. We thought that everything was over when suddenly a black sloth bear came out panting in the hot sun.

Now I will not shoot a sloth bear wantedly, but unfortunately for the poor beast, one of my companions did not feel the same way about it and promptly shot the bear on the spot.

As we watched the fallen animal, we were surprised to see that the black fur on its back moved and left the prostrate body. Then we saw it was a baby bear that had been riding on its mother's back when the sudden shot had killed her. The little creature ran around its prostrate parent, making a pitiful noise. I ran up to it to attempt a capture. It scooted into the sugarcane field. Following it with my companions, I was at last able to grab it by the scruff of its neck while it snapped and tried to scratch me with its long, hooked claws.

We put it in one of the large jute-bags we had brought, and when I got back home, I duly presented it to my wife. She was delighted! She at once put a blue colored ribbon around its neck, and after discovering the cub was a 'boy,' she christened it Bruno.

Bruno soon took to drinking milk from a bottle. It was but a step further, and within a very few days, he started eating and drinking everything else. And everything is the right word, for he ate porridge made from any ingredients, vegetables, fruit, nuts, meat (especially pork), curry and rice regardless of condiments and chilies, bread, eggs, chocolates, sweets, pudding, ice-cream, etc. As for drink: milk, tea, coffee, lime juice, aerated water, buttermilk, beer, alcoholic liquor, and, in fact, anything liquid. It all went down with relish.

The bear became very attached to our two dogs and all the children living in and around our farm. He was left quite free in his younger days and spent his time playing, running into the kitchen, and going to sleep in our beds.

One day an accident befell him. I put down poison (barium carbonate) to kill the rats and mice that had got into my library. Bruno entered the library as he often did and ate some of the poison. Paralysis set into the extent that he could not stand on his feet. But he dragged himself on his stumps to my wife, who called me. I guessed what had happened.

Off I rushed him in the car to the vet's residence. A case of poisoning! Tame Bear—barium carbonate— what to do? Out came his medical books, and a feverish reference to index began: "What poison did you say, sir?" he asked, "Barium carbonate," I said.

"Ah yes—B—Ba—Barium Salts—Ah! Barium carbonate! Symptoms— paralysis—treatment—injections of . .. Just a minute, sir. I'll bring my syringe and the medicine." Said the doc. I dashed back to the car. Bruno was still floundering about on his stumps, but clearly, he was weakening rapidly; there was some vomiting, he was breathing heavily, with heaving flanks and gaping mouth. I was really scared and did not know what to do. I was feeling very guilty and was running in and out of the vet's house doing everything the doc asked me.

"Hold him, everybody!" In goes the hypodermic—Bruno squeals — 10 c.c. of the antidote enters his system without a drop being wasted. Ten minutes later: condition unchanged! Another 10 c.c. Injected! Ten minutes later: breathing less torturous— Bruno can move his arms and legs a little although he cannot stand yet. Thirty minutes later: Bruno gets up and has a great feed! He looks at us disdainfully, as much as to say, 'What's barium carbonate to a big black bear like me?' Bruno was still eating. I was really happy to see him recover.

The months rolled on, and Bruno had grown many times the size he was when he came. He had equaled the big dogs in height and had even outgrown them. But was just as sweet, just as mischievous, just as playful. And he was very fond of us all. Above all, he loved my wife, and she loved him too! And he could do a few tricks, too. At the command, 'Bruno, wrestle,' or 'Bruno, box,' he vigorously tackled anyone who came forward for a rough and tumble. Give him a stick and say 'Bruno, hold the gun,' and he pointed the stick at you. Ask him, 'Bruno, where's baby?' and he immediately produced and cradled affectionately a stump of wood which he had carefully concealed in his straw bed. But because of the neighborhoods' and our renters' children, poor Bruno, had to be kept chained most of the time.

Then my son and I advised my wife and friends advised her, too, to give Bruno to the zoo. He was getting too big to keep at home. After some weeks of such advice, she at last consented. Hastily, and before she could change her mind, a letter was written to the curator of the zoo. Did he want a tame bear for his collection? He replied, "Yes." The zoo sent a cage in a truck, a distance of hundred – eighty – seven miles, and Bruno was packed off. We all missed him greatly, but in a sense, we were relieved. My wife was inconsolable. She wept and fretted. For the first few days, she would not eat a thing. Then she wrote a number of letters to the curator. How was Bruno? Back came the replies, "Well, but fretting; he refuses food too."

After that, friends visiting the zoo were begged to make a point of seeing how Bruno was getting along. They reported that he was well but looked very thin and sad. All the keepers at the zoo said he was fretting. For three months, I managed to restrain my wife from visiting the zoo. Then she said one day, "I must see Bruno. Either you take me by car, or I will go myself by bus or train myself." So I took her by car. Friends had conjectured that the bear would not recognize her. I had thought so too. But while she was yet some yards from his cage, Bruno saw her and recognized her. He howled with happiness. She ran up to him, petted him through the bars, and he stood on his head in delight.

For the next three hours, she would not leave that cage. She gave him tea, lemonade, cakes, ice cream, and whatnot. Then 'closing time' came and we had to leave. My wife cried bitterly; Bruno cried bitterly; even the hardened curator and the keepers felt depressed. As for me, I had reconciled myself to what I knew was going to happen next.

"Oh please, sir," she asked the curator, "may I have my Bruno back"? Hesitantly, he answered, "Madam, he belongs to the zoo and is Government property now. I cannot give away Government property. But if my boss, the superintendent, agrees, certainly, you may have him back."

There followed the return journey home and a visit to the superintendent's office. A tearful pleading: "Bruno and I are both fretting for each other. Will you please give him back to me?" He was a kind-hearted man and consented. Not only that, but he wrote to the curator, telling him to lend us a cage for transporting the bear back home.

Back we went to the zoo again, armed with the superintendent's letter. Bruno was driven into a small cage and hoisted on top of the car; the cage was tied securely, and a slow and careful return journey back home was accomplished.

Once home, a squad of workers were engaged for special work around our yard. An island was made for Bruno. It was twenty feet long and fifteen feet wide and was surrounded by a dry moat, six feet wide and seven feet deep. A wooden box that once housed fowls was brought and put on the island for Bruno to sleep in at night. Straw was placed inside to keep him warm, and his 'baby,' the gnarled stump, along with his 'gun,' the piece of bamboo, both of which had been sentimentally preserved since he had been sent away to the zoo, were put back for him to play with. In a few days, the workers hoisted the cage on to the island, and Bruno was released. He was delighted; standing on his hind legs, he pointed his 'gun' and cradled his 'baby.' My wife spent hours sitting on a chair there while he sat on her lap. He was fifteen months old and pretty heavy too!

The way my wife reaches the island and leaves it is interesting. I have tied a rope to the over-hanging branch of a maple tree with a loop at its end. Putting one foot in the loop, she kicks off with the other, to bridge the six-foot gap that constitutes the width of the surrounding moat. The return journey back is made the same way.

But who can say now that a sloth bear has no sense of affection, no memory, and no individual characteristics?

5. Which of the following would make the best alternate title for this selection?

Ⓐ The Pet
Ⓑ Hungry for Love
Ⓒ The Author's Wife
Ⓓ The Animal in the Zoo

6. What is this story mostly about?

Ⓐ about having a bear as a pet and how to care for it
Ⓑ about the bond that the bear and the author's wife shared
Ⓒ about rescuing a bear
Ⓓ about animals

7. What is the central idea of this portion of the selection? Circle the correct answer choice.

Ⓐ Bruno eats rat poison, but doesn't die.
Ⓑ An accident almost causes the narrator's family to lose its pet.
Ⓒ A vet treats a pet bear.
Ⓓ The narrator feels guilty about accidentally poisoning his pet bear.

Jane Eyre (Excerpt)
by Charlotte Bronte

Read the story below and answer the questions that follow.

The red-room was a square chamber, very seldom slept in, I might say never indeed, unless when a chance influx of visitors at Gateshead Hall rendered it necessary to turn to account all the accommodation it contained: yet it was one of the largest and stateliest chambers in the mansion. A bed supported on massive pillars of mahogany, hung with curtains of deep red damask, stood out like a tabernacle in the centre; the two large windows, with their blinds always drawn down, were half shrouded in festoons and falls of similar drapery; the carpet was red; the table at the foot of the bed was covered with a crimson cloth; the walls were a soft fawn color with a blush of pink in it; the wardrobe, the toilet-table, the chairs were of darkly polished old mahogany. Out of these deep surrounding shades rose high, and glared white, the piled-up mattresses and pillows of the bed, spread with a snowy Marseilles counterpane. Scarcely less prominent was an ample cushioned easy-chair near the head of the bed, also white, with a footstool before it; and looking, as I thought, like a pale throne.

This room was chill because it seldom had a fire; it was silent, because remote from the nursery and kitchen; solemn because it was known to be so seldom entered. The housemaid alone came here on Saturdays, to wipe from the mirrors and the furniture a week's quiet dust: and Mrs. Reed herself, at far intervals, visited it to review the contents of a certain secret drawer in the wardrobe, where were stored divers parchments, her jewel-casket, and a miniature of her deceased husband; and in those last words lies the secret of the red-room--the spell which kept it so lonely in spite of its grandeur.

8. Which sentence best summarizes the description of this room?

Ⓐ It was a cold, quiet room.
Ⓑ The cold, dusty bedroom had pinkish walls, a fireplace, a large bed, several chairs, and a wardrobe.
Ⓒ The room was dusty and abandoned.
Ⓓ The room was quiet, lonely and cold and was dominated by a large bed and several red chairs.

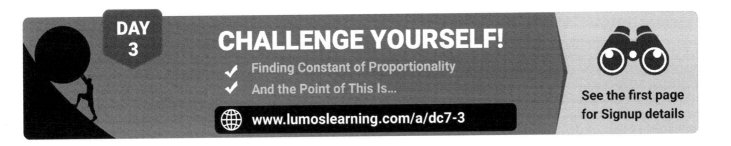

1. 3 hats cost a total of $18. Which equation describes the total cost, C, in terms of the number of hats, n?

Ⓐ C = 3n
Ⓑ C = 6n
Ⓒ C = 0.5n
Ⓓ 3C = n

2. Use the data in the table to give an equation to represent the proportional relationship.

x	y
0.5	7
1	14
1.5	21
2	28

Ⓐ y = 14x
Ⓑ y = 7x
Ⓒ 7y = x
Ⓓ 21y = x

3. Kelli has purchased a membership at the gym for the last four months. She has paid the same amount each month, and her total cost so far has been $100. What equation expresses the proportional relationship of the cost and month?

Ⓐ C = 100m
Ⓑ C = 50m
Ⓒ C = 4m
Ⓓ C = 25m

4. Solve each proportion for x and match it with the correct solution for x.

	x = 9	x = 10	x = 7
$\dfrac{x}{15} = \dfrac{3}{5}$	☐	☐	☐
$\dfrac{16}{14} = \dfrac{8}{x}$	☐	☐	☐
$\dfrac{4}{20} = \dfrac{2}{x}$	☐	☐	☐
$\dfrac{75}{x} = \dfrac{50}{6}$	☐	☐	☐

Tryouts

Read the story below and answer the questions that follow.

For years, Sam had dreamed of being the best tennis player in the world. He went to tennis practice every single morning and every single night. He spent every summer at tennis camp, and he gave up long weekends at the beach to work on his game. Now, it seemed his hard work was finally paying off: he was invited to try out for the state tennis team!

Still, there was something that was bothering Sam. The tryouts for the tennis team were on the same day as his mom's birthday, and he knew his family was planning a huge surprise party for her. He didn't want to hurt his mom's feelings by missing the party, but he also didn't want to miss his one shot at being a champion tennis player just because the tryouts were on his mom's birthday. He was in a quandary; he didn't know what to do.

For days, Sam went to bed worrying about the decision. If he went to the tryout, he worried he would seem selfish. If he stayed home, he would miss his one big shot at making the state team. In fact, despite the honor of being invited to try out, he hadn't even told his family about the opportunity. He was so stressed about making the decision of whether to go that he couldn't even think about sharing the news.

Weeks went by, and Sam was making no progress. Every day his coach asked him if he was ready for the tryout, and Sam couldn't even respond. Finally, Sam couldn't bear the stress any longer. He decided to talk to his grandfather about his predicament.

"You know, your mom wants you to be happy," he told Sam. "It would be a great birthday present for her to know you are making your dream come true."

Sam had never thought of it that way before, and after talking to his grandfather, he knew what he had to do. He immediately went home and sat down with his parents to let them know about the opportunity to try out for the state team. His parents were so excited that when he told them, apologetically, what day the tryouts were, and they were so busy shrieking with excitement that he thought maybe they hadn't heard.

"But Mom, that means I'm going to miss your birthday," Sam said. "I am happy you are being so nice about it, but I still feel really bad."

"Are you kidding?" his mom asked? "This is the best present I could ask for!"

5. What is the theme of the above story?

Ⓐ family values and priorities.
Ⓑ pleasing everybody in your family
Ⓒ doing what is very important to you no matter how others feel
Ⓓ sports above all else

6. What message about relationship is this story trying to pass on to readers?

Ⓐ Friends can come and go out of each others' lives, but mother's love is permanent
Ⓑ You should always ask friends to help you with your life choices.
Ⓒ Open communication helps resolve seemingly difficult problems.
Ⓓ Thinking over a problem in a quiet place is the best way to resolve a conflict.

Moral of "The Dog and the Wolf" by Marmaduke Park

Read the poem below and answer the questions that follow.

Our neighbors sometimes seem to be
A vast deal better off than we;
Yet seldom 'tis they really are,
Since they have troubles too to bear,
Which, if the truth were really known,
Are quite as grievous as our own.

7. What is the best summary of the moral of this poem?

Ⓐ It's best to ignore those who complain.
Ⓑ Dogs and wolves will never get along.
Ⓒ Everyone else has problems too, that are likely to be grievous as yours.
Ⓓ Avoid those who look down on you.

"From "The Dog and the Wolf"
by Marmaduke Park

Read the poem below and answer the questions that follow.

A wolf there was, whose scanty fare
Had made his person lean and spare;
A dog there was, so amply fed,
His sides were plump and sleek; 'tis said
The wolf once met this prosp'rous cur,
And thus began: "Your servant, sir;
I'm pleased to see you look so well,
Though how it is I cannot tell;
I have not broke my fast to-day;
Nor have I, I'm concern'd to say,
One bone in store or expectation,
And that I call a great vexation."

8. **Part A**
   What does the wolf represent in this poem?

   Ⓐ   the basic idea of dieting
   Ⓑ   how to fast (not eat)
   Ⓒ   the basic needs of living
   Ⓓ   being a wild animal

   Part B
   What does the dog represent in this poem?

   Ⓐ   being a tamed animal
   Ⓑ   the comforts of having everything needed in life
   Ⓒ   being greedy
   Ⓓ   sharing with others

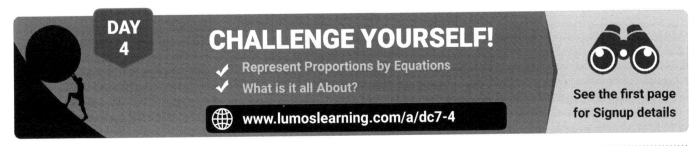

DAY 4

CHALLENGE YOURSELF!
✓ Represent Proportions by Equations
✓ What is it all About?
🌐 www.lumoslearning.com/a/dc7-4

See the first page
for Signup details

1. Which point on the graph of the straight line demonstrates that the line represents a proportion?

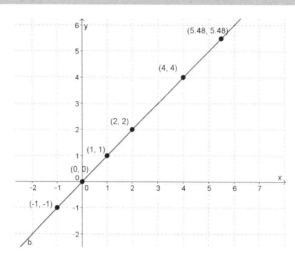

Ⓐ (2, 2)
Ⓑ (0, 0)
Ⓒ (5.48, 5.48)
Ⓓ (-1, -1)

2. Which point on the graph of the straight line names the unit rate of the proportional relationship?

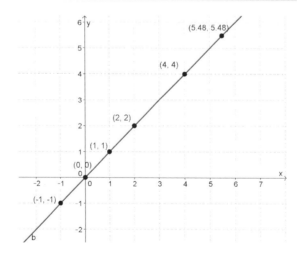

Ⓐ (1, 1)
Ⓑ (0, 0)
Ⓒ (2, 2)
Ⓓ (4, 4)

3. The graph shows the relationship between the number of classes in the school and the total number of students. How many students are there per class?

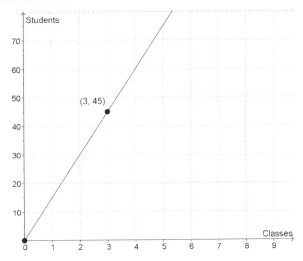

Ⓐ   45 students
Ⓑ   3 students
Ⓒ   135 students
Ⓓ   15 students

4. What do the points on the graph mean? Select all the correct answers.

Ⓐ   After 2 weeks, you have saved $94
Ⓑ   After 94 weeks, you have saved $2
Ⓒ   After 10 weeks, you have saved $94
Ⓓ   After 4 weeks, you have saved $188
Ⓔ   After 0 weeks, you have saved $10

"The Lament"
by Sravani

Read the story below and answer the questions that follow.

It is twilight. Thick wet snow is slowly twirling around the newly lighted street lamps and lying in soft hin layers on roofs, on horses' backs, on people's shoulders and hats. The cab driver, Iona Potapov, is quite white and looks like a phantom: he is bent double as far as a human body can bend double; he is seated on his box; he never makes a move. If a whole snowdrift fell on him, it seems as if he would not find it necessary to shake it off. His little horse is also quite white, and remains motionless; its immobility, its angularity, and its straight wooden-looking legs, even close by, give it the appearance of a gingerbread horse worth a kopek. It is, no doubt, plunged in deep thought. If you were snatched from the plough, from your usual gray surroundings, and were thrown into this slough full of monstrous lights, unceasing noise and hurrying people, you too would find it difficult not to think. Iona and his little horse have not moved from their place for a long while. They left their yard before dinner and, up to now, not a fare. The evening mist is descending over the town, the white lights of the lamps are replacing brighter rays, and the hubbub of the street is getting louder.

'Cabby for Viborg Way!' suddenly hears Iona. 'Cabby!'
Iona jumps and, through his snow-covered eyelashes, sees an officer in a greatcoat, with his hood over his head.

'Viborg way!' the officer repeats. 'Are you asleep, eh? Viborg way!'
With a nod of assent, Iona picks up the reins, in

consequence of which layers of snow slip off the horse's back and neck. The officer seats himself in the sleigh, the cab driver smacks his lips to encourage his horse, stretches out his neck like a swan, sits up and, more from habit than necessity, brandishes his whip. The little horse also stretches its neck, bends its wooden-looking legs, and makes a move undecidedly.

'What are you doing, werewolf!' is the exclamation Iona hears from the dark mass moving to and fro, as soon as they have started. 'Where the devil are you going? To the r-r-right!'

'You do not know how to drive. Keep to the right!' calls the officer angrily. A coachman from a private carriage swears at him; a passerby, who has run across the road and rubbed his shoulder against the horse's nose, looks at him furiously as he sweeps the snow from his sleeve. Iona shifts about on his seat as if he was on needles, moves his elbows as if he were trying to keep his equilibrium, and gasps about like someone suffocating, who does not understand why and wherefore he is there.

'What scoundrels they all are!' jokes the officer; 'one would think they had all entered into an agreement to jostle you or fall under your horse.'
Iona looks around at the officer and moves his lips. He evidently wants to say something but the only sound that issues is a snuffle.

'What?' asks the officer. Iona twists his mouth

into a smile and, with an effort, says hoarsely: 'My son,
Barin, died this week.' 'Hm! What did he die of?'

Iona turns with his whole body towards his fare and says: 'And who knows! They say high fever. He
was three days in the hospital and then died...

God's will be done.'

"Turn round! The devil!' sounds from the darkness. 'Have you popped off, old doggie, eh? Use your
eyes!'
'Go on, go on,' says the officer, 'otherwise we shall not get there by tomorrow. Hurry up a bit!'

5. What event that occurred before the story begins, influences the way the character Iona acts in this story?

Ⓐ The death of his son
Ⓑ The winter storm
Ⓒ The officer's harsh comments
Ⓓ Iona's wife's sickness

6. Based on the plot of this story, what can you assume was The Lament mentioned in the title?

Ⓐ The officer had to reach Viborg urgently.
Ⓑ Grief made the cabby confused.
Ⓒ The people were sad because the cabby was not driving carefully.
Ⓓ The horse was lost.

Best Friend

Read the story below and answer the questions that follow.

Ever since they were kids, Julie and Max had been best friends. They went to kindergarten together. They went to summer camp together. They hung out together every weekend. But suddenly, things between the two had started to change.

Max had started playing on the football team and didn't have much time for Julie anymore. He was always busy, and he never seemed to make it to study hall, where the two used to swap stories about their favorite (or least favorite) teachers. In class, Julie noticed that Max never seemed to have his homework done on time anymore. She even noticed that he got a 'D' on his last paper. She knew something was going on with him – but what?

At first, Julie decided to play it cool and see how things went. She tried waiting in the hall for Max after class to see if she could ask if he was OK. But days went by, and he never had time to stop. He'd rush right past her in the hall, only to leave her feeling even worse about what was happening between them.

Even though she wasn't sure she could handle the situation herself, Julie didn't want to talk to her parents because she was afraid they would tell her not to hang out with Max anymore. She barely saw him as it was, so she knew it would just make things worse if her parents didn't approve of him. She didn't want to tell Max's parents either because she didn't want him to get in trouble. Still, it seemed like something needed to change.

Julie decided to go to one of her school counselors and let her know she was concerned. When she walked into Mrs. Smith's room, she was surprised to see that Max was already sitting there. "I'm sorry, I'll come back," Julie said.

"No, stay," said Max. "Maybe you can help."

Julie was surprised to find that Max had visited the counselor's office for the same reason she had: he was starting to feel overwhelmed with all of the things he was supposed to be doing as a student, an athlete, and a friend. He needed some guidance on how to determine what truly mattered and how to divide his time between all of the things that were important to him.

When she realized that Max was still the same old Max (just a little more stressed), Julie was relieved. She was also happy to know that he had come to a conclusion on his own, without her having to talk to someone else about it. She decided it was a sign they were both growing up.

7. How does Max playing football affect his relationship with Julie in this story?

- Ⓐ It brings the two of them closer together.
- Ⓑ It gives the two something to talk about during study hall.
- Ⓒ It makes Julie jealous.
- Ⓓ It keeps the two of them from spending time together.

Summer Trip

Read the story below and answer the questions that follow.

"Juan!" Jacob called out excitedly to his best friend as he ran up to him in the hallway. "You are never going to believe what just happened in Mrs. Smith's class!"

"What, Jake?" Juan was a little unsure of what type of news his friend could have. Jacob had a tendency to get excited about the strangest things.

"She told us we get to go to Washington D.C., and New York City this summer!"

Juan stared at his friend in astonishment. He had always wanted to go to New York City.

"No way!" he exclaimed.

"I'm serious! We get to travel as a class, stay in hotels, and visit the Capitol building as well as the White House."

"What about seeing a Broadway play?" Juan asked. "I have always wanted to see The Lion King on stage. My sister saw it when she was in high school, and she said it was amazing!"

"Who cares?" Jacob asked with an incredulous look on his face. "We might get to see the President in the White House!"

Juan just shook his head at his friend. "Uh. I don't think he just walks around the White House."

"You never know. But it won't matter if our parents do not agree to let us go."

Juan knew Jacob was right, and more than likely, his parents would not want him to go. They never trusted him to do anything without one of them going as well. Silence filled the air between the two friends for several seconds just before the warning bell sounded.

Each was lost in his own thoughts, planning how they could convince their parents to let them go.

"Let's come up with a plan to ask them while we are at lunch," Juan suggested.

Jacob agreed immediately. "That's a great idea! I'll see you then."

8. Which event occurred third in the story?

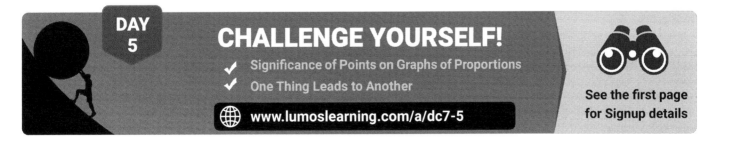

LEARN SIGN LANGUAGE

What is American Sign Language?

American Sign Language (ASL) is a complete, complex language that employs signs made by moving the hands combined with facial expressions and postures of the body. It is the primary language of many North Americans who are deaf and is one of several communication options used by people who are deaf or hard-of-hearing.

Where did ASL originate?

The exact beginnings of ASL are not clear, but some suggest that it arose more than 200 years ago from the intermixing of local sign languages and French Sign Language (LSF, or Langue des Signes Française). Today's ASL includes some elements of LSF plus the original local sign languages, which over the years have melded and changed into a rich, complex, and mature language. Modern ASL and modern LSF are distinct languages and, while they still contain some similar signs, can no longer be understood by each other's users

Source: https://www.nidcd.nih.gov/health/american-sign-language

WHY SHOULD ONE LEARN SIGN LANGUAGE?

ENRICH YOUR COGNITIVE SKILLS
Sign language can enrich the cognitive development of a child. Since, different cognitive skills can be acquired as a child, learning sign language, can be implemented with practice and training in early childhood.

MAKE NEW FRIENDS
You could communicate better with the hearing-impaired people you meet, if you know the sign language, it is easier to understand and communicate effectively.

VOLUNTEER
Use your ASL skills to interpret as a volunteer. volunteers can help in making a real difference in people's lives, with their time, effort and commitment.

BILINGUAL
If you are monolingual, here is an opportunity to become bilingual, with a cause.

PRIVATE CHAT
It would be useful to converse with a friend or in a group without anyone understanding, what you are up to.

LEARN SIGN LANGUAGE

 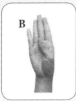 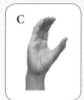 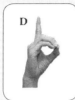

✔ Sign language is fun if it is practiced with friends

✔ Partner with your friends or family members and try the following activities

ACTIVITY

1. Communicate the following to your friend using the ASL.
   - USA
   - ASL

   If your friend hasn't mastered the ASL yet, give the above alphabet chart to your friend.

2. Try saying your name in ASL using the hand gestures.

3. Have your friend communicate a funny word using ASL and you try to read it without the help of the chart. List the words you tried below.

LET'S LEARN SOME WORDS

RED	ORANGE	YELLOW	EAT	DRINK	MORE

GREEN	PURPLE	BLUE	PLEASE	THANK YOU	SORRY

LET'S LEARN THE NUMBERS

   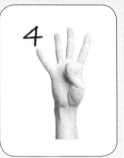 

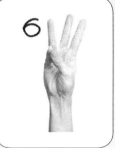    

THIS WEEK'S ONLINE ACTIVITIES

✔ Reading Assignment ✔ Vocabulary Practice
✔ Write Your Summer Diary

🌐 www.lumoslearning.com/a/slh7-8

See the first page for Signup details

WEEKLY FUN SUMMER PHOTO CONTEST

 Take a picture of your summer fun activity and share it on Twitter or Instagram

Use the #SummerLearning mention

@LumosLearning on	@lumos.learning on
🐦 **Twitter**	📷 **Instagram**

 Tag friends and increase your chances of winning the contest.

PARTICIPATE AND STAND A CHANCE TO WIN $50 AMAZON GIFT CARD!

WEEK 2
SUMMER PRACTICE

1. What value of x will make these two expressions equivalent?

$$\frac{-3}{7} \text{ and } \frac{x}{21}$$

   Ⓐ x = -3
   Ⓑ x = 7
   Ⓒ x = 9
   Ⓓ x = -9

2. If p varies proportionally to s, and p = 10 when s = 2, which of the following equations correctly models this relationship?

   Ⓐ p = 5s
   Ⓑ p = 10s
   Ⓒ s = 10p
   Ⓓ 2s = 10p

3. Solve for x, if $\frac{72}{108}$ and $\frac{x}{54}$ are equivalent.

   Ⓐ x = 18
   Ⓑ x = 36
   Ⓒ x = 54
   Ⓓ x = 24

4. What is 30% of 64? Enter your answer in the box given below.

   _____

"Scouting for Boys"
(Excerpt)

Read the story below and answer the questions that follow.

"Hi! Stop Thief!" shouted old Blenkinsopp as he rushed out of his little store near the village.

"He's stolen my sugar. Stop him."

Stop whom? There was nobody in sight running away, "Who stole it?" asked the policeman.

"I don't know, but a whole bag of sugar is missing. It was there only a few minutes ago." The policeman tried to track the thief, but it looked a pretty impossible job for him to single out the tracks of the thief from among dozens of other footprints about the store. However, he presently started off hopefully, at a jog-trot, away out into the bush. In some places, he went over the hard stony ground, but he never checked his pace, although no footmarks could be seen. People wondered how he could possibly find the trail. Still, he trotted on. Old Blenkinsopp was feeling the heat and the pace At length, he suddenly stopped and cast around, having evidently lost the trail. Then a grin came on his face as he pointed with his thumb over

his shoulder up the tree near which he was standing.

There, concealed among the branches, they saw a young man with the missing bag of sugar. How had the policeman spotted him? His sharp eyes had detected some grains of sugar sparkling in the dust. The bag leaked, leaving a slight trail of these grains. He followed that trail, and when it came to an end in the bush, he·noticed a string of ants going up a tree. They were after the sugar, and so was he, and between them, they brought about the capture of the thief.

Old Blenkinsopp was so pleased that he promptly opened the bag and spilled a lot of the sugar on the ground as a reward to the ants.

He also appreciated the policeman for his cleverness in using his eyes to see the grains of sugar and the ants, and in using his wits to know why the ants were climbing the tree.

---

5. Based on the details in this story, where can you infer where the story begins (setting)?

Ⓐ a store
Ⓑ a house
Ⓒ a bakery
Ⓓ a police station

"The Lament"
by Sravani

Read the story below and answer the questions that follow.

It is twilight. Thick wet snow is slowly twirling around the newly lighted street lamps and lying in soft thin layers on roofs, on horses' backs, on people's shoulders and hats. The cab driver, Iona Potapov, is quite white and looks like a phantom: he is bent double as far as a human body can bend double; he is seated on his box; he never makes a move. If a whole snowdrift fell on him, it seems as if he would not find it necessary to shake it off. His little horse is also quite white, and remains motionless; its immobility, its angularity, and its straight wooden-looking legs, even close by, give it the appearance of a gingerbread horse worth a kopek. It is, no doubt, plunged in deep thought. If you were snatched from the plough, from your usual gray surroundings, and were thrown into this slough full of monstrous lights, unceasing noise and hurrying people, you too would find it difficult not to think.

Iona and his little horse have not moved from their place for a long while. They left their yard before dinner and, up to now, not a fare. The evening mist is descending over the town, the white lights of the lamps are replacing brighter rays, and the hubbub of the street is getting louder.
'Cabby for Viborg Way!' suddenly hears Iona. 'Cabby!'
Iona jumps and, through his snow-covered eyelashes, sees an officer in a greatcoat, with his hood over his head.
'Viborg way!' the officer repeats. 'Are you asleep, eh? Viborg way!'
With a nod of assent, Iona picks up the reins, in consequence of which layers of snow slip off the horse's back and neck. The officer seats himself in the sleigh, the cab driver smacks his lips to encourage his horse, stretches out his neck like a swan, sits up and, more from habit than necessity, brandishes his whip. The little horse also stretches its neck, bends its wooden-looking legs, and makes a move undecidedly.

'What are you doing, werewolf!' is the exclamation Iona hears from the dark mass moving to and fro, as soon as they have started.
'Where the devil are you going? To the r-r-right!'
'You do not know how to drive. Keep to the right!' calls the officer angrily. A coachman from a private carriage swears at him; a passerby, who has run across the road and rubbed his shoulder against he horse's nose, looks at him furiously as he sweeps the snow from his sleeve. Iona shifts about on his seat as if he was on needles, moves his elbows as if he were trying to keep his equilibrium, and gasps about like someone suffocating, who does not understand why and wherefore he is there.

'What scoundrels they all are!' jokes the officer; 'one would think they had all entered into an agreement to jostle you or fall under your horse.'
Iona looks around at the officer and moves his lips. He evidently wants to say something but the only sound that issues is a snuffle.

'What?' asks the officer.
Iona twists his mouth into a smile and, with an effort, says hoarsely:

'My son, Barin, died this week.' '
'Hm! What did he die of?'
Iona turns with his whole body towards his fare and says: 'And who knows! They say high fever. He was three days in the hospital and then died... God's will be done.'

"Turn round! The devil!' sounds from the darkness. 'Have you popped off, old doggie, eh? Use your eyes!'
'Go on, go on,' says the officer, 'otherwise we shall not get there by tomorrow. Hurry up a bit!'

6. Which detail in the above passage tells us this story is set in the winter?

Ⓐ It is twilight.
Ⓑ His little horse is also quite white, and remains motionless;
Ⓒ A thick wet snow is slowly twirling around the newly lighted street lamps and lying in soft thin layers on roofs, on horses' backs, on people's shoulders and hats.
Ⓓ The cabdriver, Iona Potapov, is quite white and looks like a phantom: he is bent double as far as a human body can bend double;

7. What details in the above story tell us that this story's setting is Russia?

Ⓐ The name of the cab driver, Iona Potapov.
Ⓑ A police officer asks for a cab ride.
Ⓒ It is snowing heavily.
Ⓓ The name of the place the officer wants to go.

"The Fox and the Stork"
From Aesop's Fables

Read the story below and answer the questions that follow.

At one time, the Fox and the Stork were on visiting terms and seemed very good friends. So the Fox invited the Stork to dinner, and for a joke, put nothing before her but some soup in a very shallow dish. This the Fox could easily lap up, but the Stork could only wet the end of her long bill in it and left the meal as hungry as when she began. "I am sorry, said the Fox, "the soup is not to your liking."

"Pray, do not apologize," said the Stork. "I hope you will return this visit and come and dine with me soon." So a day was appointed when the Fox should visit the Stork; but when they were seated at the table all that was for their dinner was contained in a very long-necked jar with a narrow mouth, in which the Fox could not insert his snout, so all he could manage to do was to lick the outside of the jar.

"The Fox and the Stork"
From Aesop's Fables

Read the story below and answer the questions that follow.

At one time, the Fox and the Stork were on visiting terms and seemed very good friends. So the Fox invited the Stork to dinner, and for a joke, put nothing before her but some soup in a very shallow dish. This the Fox could easily lap up, but the Stork could only wet the end of her long bill in it and left the meal as hungry as when she began. "I am sorry, said the Fox, "the soup is not to your liking."

"Pray, do not apologize," said the Stork. "I hope you will return this visit and come and dine with me soon." So a day was appointed when the Fox should visit the Stork; but when they were seated at the table all that was for their dinner was contained in a very long-necked jar with a narrow mouth, in which the Fox could not insert his snout, so all he could manage to do was to lick the outside of the jar.

8. Part A
What is the setting of this story?

Ⓐ The Fox and the Stork's homes
Ⓑ The 100 Acre Wood
Ⓒ A castle
Ⓓ A pond

Part B
Based on the events happening in the poem, when does poem take place?

Ⓐ At breakfast
Ⓑ In the evening
Ⓒ Snack time
Ⓓ Tea time

DAY 1

CHALLENGE YOURSELF!
✓ Applying Ratios and Percents
✓ When and Where?

🌐 www.lumoslearning.com/a/dc7-6

See the first page
for Signup details

1. **Evaluate: 25 + 2.005 - 7.253 - 2.977**

   Ⓐ -16.775
   Ⓑ 16.775
   Ⓒ 167.75
   Ⓓ 1.6775

2. **Add and/or subtract as indicated :** $-3\dfrac{4}{5} + 9\dfrac{7}{10} - 2\dfrac{11}{20} =$

   Ⓐ $3\dfrac{7}{20}$

   Ⓑ $4\dfrac{7}{10}$

   Ⓒ $4\dfrac{9}{20}$

   Ⓓ $3\dfrac{1}{20}$

3. **Linda and Carrie made a trip from their hometown to a city about 200 miles away to attend a friend's wedding. The following chart shows their distances, stops and times. What part of their total trip did they spend driving?**

3hr	driving
15 min	rest stop
$1\dfrac{1}{2}$ hr	driving
1 hr	rest stop
20 min	driving

   Ⓐ $\dfrac{4}{5}$

   Ⓑ $\dfrac{2}{5}$

   Ⓒ $\dfrac{58}{73}$

   Ⓓ $\dfrac{99}{100}$

4. Read the number sentences below and match it with the correct associated property.

	Associative Property of Addition	Inverse Property of Addition	Identity Property of Addition
$\frac{2}{5}+0=\frac{2}{5}$	○	○	○
$\frac{1}{4}\left(\frac{2}{3}+\frac{7}{8}\right)=\left(\frac{1}{4}+\frac{2}{3}\right)+\frac{7}{8}$	○	○	○
$\frac{6}{7}+ - \frac{6}{7}=0$	○	○	○

"Bruno the Bear"
From A Bond of Love

Read the story below and answer the questions that follow.

I WILL begin with Bruno, my wife's pet sloth bear. I got him for her by accident. Two years ago, we were passing through the cornfields near a small town in Iowa. People were driving away the wild pigs from the fields by shooting at them. Some were shot, and some escaped. We thought that everything was over when suddenly a black sloth bear came out panting in the hot sun. Now I will not shoot a sloth bear wantonly, but unfortunately for the poor beast, one of my companions did not feel the same way about it and promptly shot the bear on the spot.

As we watched the fallen animal, we were surprised to see that the black fur on its back moved and left the prostrate body. Then we saw it was a baby bear that had been riding on its mother's back when the sudden shot had killed her. The little creature ran around its prostrate parent, making a pitiful noise. I ran up to it to attempt a capture. It scooted into the sugarcane field. Following it with my companions, I was at last able to grab it by the scruff of its neck while it snapped and tried to scratch me with its long, hooked claws. We put it in one of the large jute-bags we had brought, and when I got back home, I duly presented it to my wife. She was delighted! She at once put a blue colored ribbon around its neck, and after discovering the cub was a 'boy,' she christened it Bruno. Bruno soon took to drinking milk from a bottle. It was but a step further, and within a very few days, he started eating and drinking everything else. And everything is the right word, for he ate porridge made from any ingredients, vegetables, fruit, nuts, meat (especially pork), curry and rice regardless of condiments and chilies, bread, eggs, chocolates, sweets, pudding, ice-cream, etc., etc., etc. As for drink: milk, tea, coffee, lime juice, aerated water, buttermilk, beer, alcoholic liquor, and, in fact, anything liquid. It all went down with relish. The bear became very attached to our two dogs and to all the children living in and around our farm. He was left quite free in his younger days and spent his time playing, running into the kitchen, and going to sleep in our beds. One day an accident befell him. I put down poison (barium carbonate) to kill the rats and mice that had got into my library. Bruno entered the library as he often did and ate some of the poison. Paralysis set into the extent that he could not stand on his feet. But he dragged himself on his stumps to my wife, who called me. I guessed what had happened. Off I rushed him in the car to the vet's residence. A case of poisoning! Tame Bear—barium carbonate—what to do? Out came his medical books, and a feverish reference to index began: "What poison did you say, sir?" he asked, "Barium carbonate," I said. "Ah yes—B—Ba—Barium Salts—Ah! Barium carbonate! Symptoms— paralysis— treatment—injections of . .. Just a minute, sir. I'll bring my syringe and the medicine." Said the doc. I dashed back to the car. Bruno was still floundering about on his stumps, but clearly, he was weakening rapidly; there was some vomiting, he was breathing heavily, with heaving flanks and gaping mouth. I was really scared and did not know what to do. I was feeling very guilty and was running in and out of the vet's house doing everything the doc asked me.

"Hold him, everybody!" In goes the hypodermic—Bruno squeals — 10 c.c. of the antidote enters his system without a drop being wasted. Ten minutes later: condition unchanged! Another 10 c.c. Injected! Ten minutes later: breathing less torturous— Bruno can move his arms and legs a little although he cannot stand yet. Thirty minutes later: Bruno gets up and has a great feed! He looks at us disdainfully, as much as to say, 'What's barium carbonate to a big black bear like me?' Bruno was still eating. I was really happy to see him recover. The months rolled on, and Bruno had grown many times the size he was when he came. He had equaled the big dogs in height and had even outgrown them. But was just as sweet, just as mischievous, just as playful. And he was very fond of us all. Above all, he loved my wife, and she loved him too! And he could do a few tricks, too. At the command, 'Bruno, wrestle,' or 'Bruno, box,' he vigorously tackled anyone who came forward for a rough and tumble. Give him a stick and say 'Bruno, hold the gun,' and he pointed the stick at you. Ask him, 'Bruno, where's baby?' and he immediately produced and cradled affectionately a stump of wood which he had carefully concealed in his straw bed. But because of the neighborhoods' and our renters' children, poor Bruno, had to be kept chained most of the time. Then my son and I advised my wife and friends advised her, too, to give Bruno to the zoo. He was getting too big to keep at home. After some weeks of such advice, she at last consented. Hastily, and before she could change her mind, a letter was written to the curator of the zoo. Did he want a tame bear for his collection? He replied, "Yes." The zoo sent a cage in a truck, a distance of hundred – eighty – seven miles, and Bruno was packed off. We all missed him greatly, but in a sense, we were relieved. My wife was inconsolable. She wept and fretted. For the first few days, she would not eat a thing. Then she wrote a number of letters to the curator. How was Bruno? Back came the replies, "Well, but fretting; he refuses food too." After that, friends visiting the zoo were begged to make a point of seeing how Bruno was getting along. They reported that he was well but looked very thin and sad. All the keepers at the zoo said he was fretting. For three months, I managed to restrain my wife from visiting the zoo. Then she said one day, "I must see Bruno. Either you take me by car, or I will go myself by bus or train myself." So I took her by car. Friends had conjectured that the bear would not recognize her. I had thought so too. But while she was yet some yards from his cage, Bruno saw her and recognized her. He howled with happiness. She ran up to him, petted him through the bars, and he stood on his head in delight. For the next three hours, she would not leave that cage. She gave him tea, lemonade, cakes, ice cream, and whatnot. Then 'closing time' came and we had to leave. My wife cried bitterly; Bruno cried bitterly; even the hardened curator and the keepers felt depressed. As for me, I had reconciled myself to what I knew was going to happen next.

"Oh please, sir," she asked the curator, "may I have my Bruno back"? Hesitantly, he answered, "Madam, he belongs to the zoo and is Government property now. I cannot give away Government property. But if my boss, the superintendent, agrees, certainly, you may have him back." There followed the return journey home and a visit to the superintendent's office. A tearful pleading: "Bruno and I are both fretting for each other. Will you please give him back to me?" He was a kind-hearted man and consented. Not only that, but he wrote to the curator, telling him to lend us a cage for transporting the bear back home. Back we went to the zoo again, armed with the superintendent's letter. Bruno was driven into a small cage and hoisted on top of the car; the cage was tied securely, and a slow and careful return journey back home was accomplished. Once

home, a squad of workers were engaged for special work around our yard. An island was made for Bruno. It was twenty feet long and fifteen feet wide and was surrounded by a dry moat, six feet wide and seven feet deep.

A wooden box that once housed fowls was brought and put on the island for Bruno to sleep in at night. Straw was placed inside to keep him warm, and his 'baby,' the gnarled stump, along with his 'gun,' the piece of bamboo, both of which had been sentimentally preserved since he had been sent away to the zoo, were put back for him to play with. In a few days, the workers hoisted the cage on to the island, and Bruno was released. He was delighted; standing on his hind legs, he pointed his 'gun' and cradled his 'baby.' My wife spent hours sitting on a chair there while he sat on her lap. He was fifteen months old and pretty heavy too! The way my wife reaches the island and leaves it is interesting. I have tied a rope to the overhanging branch of a maple tree with a loop at its end. Putting one foot in the loop, she kicks off with the other, to bridge the six-foot gap that constitutes the width of the surrounding moat. The return journey back is made the same way. But who can say now that a sloth bear has no sense of affection, no memory, and no individual characteristics?

5. What motivated the narrator to keep Bruno chained up?

Ⓐ because he had grown big
Ⓑ because he was very playful and this scared some of the children in the neighborhood
Ⓒ because he was very dangerous
Ⓓ because he was a bear

Best Friend

Read the story below and answer the questions that follow.

Ever since they were kids, Julie and Max had been best friends. They went to kindergarten together. They went to summer camp together. They hung out together every weekend. But suddenly, things between the two had started to change.

Max had started playing on the football team and didn't have much time for Julie anymore. He was always busy, and he never seemed to make it to study hall, where the two used to swap stories about their favorite (or least favorite) teachers. In class, Julie noticed that Max never seemed to have his homework done on time anymore. She even noticed that he got a 'D' on his last paper. She knew something was going on with him – but what?

At first, Julie decided to play it cool and see how things went. She tried waiting in the hall for Max after class to see if she could ask if he was OK. But days went by, and he never had time to stop. He'd rush right past her in the hall, only to leave her feeling even worse about what was happening between them.

Even though she wasn't sure she could handle the situation herself, Julie didn't want to talk to her parents because she was afraid they would tell her not to hang out with Max anymore. She barely saw him as it was, so she knew it would just make things worse if her parents didn't approve of him. She didn't want to tell Max's parents either because she didn't want him to get in trouble. Still, it seemed like something needed to change.

Julie decided to go to one of her school counselors and let her know she was concerned. When she walked into Mrs. Smith's room, she was surprised to see that Max was already sitting there. "I'm sorry, I'll come back," Julie said.

"No, stay," said Max. "Maybe you can help."

Julie was surprised to find that Max had visited the counselor's office for the same reason she had: he was starting to feel overwhelmed with all of the things he was supposed to be doing as a student, an athlete, and a friend. He needed some guidance on how to determine what truly mattered and how to divide his time between all of the things that were important to him.

When she realized that Max was still the same old Max (just a little more stressed), Julie was relieved. She was also happy to know that he had come to a conclusion on his own, without her having to talk to someone else about it. She decided it was a sign they were both growing up.

6. What events in the story did NOT contribute to the character of Max being overwhelmed?

- Ⓐ work commitments
- Ⓑ school commitments
- Ⓒ sports commitments
- Ⓓ parent's expectations

7. Which of the following is NOT an event in the story that leads Julie to become worried about Max?

- Ⓐ He was getting bad grades.
- Ⓑ He wasn't doing his homework.
- Ⓒ He had lost weight.
- Ⓓ He was too busy for her.

Best Friend

Read the story below and answer the questions that follow.

"Juan!" Jacob called out excitedly to his best friend as he ran up to him in the hallway. "You are never going to believe what just happened in Mrs. Smith's class!"

"What, Jake?" Juan was a little unsure of what type of news his friend could have. Jacob had a tendency to get excited about the strangest things.

"She told us we get to go to Washington D.C., and New York City this summer!"

Juan stared at his friend in astonishment. He had always wanted to go to New York City. "No way!" he exclaimed.

"I'm serious! We get to travel as a class, stay in hotels, and visit the Capitol building as well as the White House."

"What about seeing a Broadway play?" Juan asked. "I have always wanted to see The Lion King on stage. My sister saw it when she was in high school, and she said it was amazing!"

"Who cares?" Jacob asked with an incredulous look on his face. "We might get to see the President in the White House!"

Juan just shook his head at his friend. "Uh. I don't think he just walks around the White House."

"You never know. But it won't matter if our parents do not agree to let us go."

Juan knew Jacob was right, and more than likely, his parents would not want him to go. They never trusted him to do anything without one of them going as well. Silence filled the air between the two friends for several seconds just before the warning bell sounded. Each was lost in his own thoughts, planning how they could convince their parents to let them go.

"Let's come up with a plan to ask them while we are at lunch," Juan suggested.

Jacob agreed immediately. "That's a great idea! I'll see you then."

8. How did Juan know Jacob might have amazing news?

Ⓐ Jacob ran up to him in the hallway talking excitedly.
Ⓑ Jacob just came from Mrs. Smith's class and she always does cool things.
Ⓒ Jacob's brother could go as a chaperone.
Ⓓ Juan was unsure what kind of news his friend would have.

1. If p + q has a value that is exactly 1/3 less than p, what is the value of q?

   Ⓐ   −1/3
   Ⓑ   2/5
   Ⓒ   1/3
   Ⓓ   −2/5

2. What is the sum of k and the opposite of k?

   Ⓐ   2k
   Ⓑ   k + 1
   Ⓒ   0
   Ⓓ   −1

3. If p + q has a value of $\dfrac{12}{5}$, and p has a value of $\dfrac{4}{5}$, what is the value of q?

   Ⓐ $\dfrac{5}{8}$

   Ⓑ $\dfrac{8}{5}$

   Ⓒ $\dfrac{1}{3}$

   Ⓓ $\dfrac{3}{2}$

4. Solve $\dfrac{9}{14} - \dfrac{3}{14}$ and indicate it by shading the relevant boxes.

From THE HISTORY OF THE SEVEN FAMILIES OF THE LAKE PIPPLE-POPPLE. by Edward Lear

Read the story below and answer the questions that follow.

The Parrots lived upon the Soffsky-Poffsky trees, which were beautiful to behold, and covered with blue leaves; and they fed upon fruit, artichokes, and striped beetles. The Storks walked in and out of the Lake Pipple-Popple and ate frogs for breakfast and buttered toast for tea, but on account of the extreme length of their legs, they could not sit down, and so they walked about continually.

The Geese, having webs to their feet, caught quantities of flies, which they ate for dinner. The Owls anxiously looked after mice, which they caught, and made into sago-puddings. The Guinea Pigs toddled about the gardens and ate lettuces and Cheshire cheese. The Cats sate still in the sunshine and fed upon sponge biscuits. The Fishes lived in the lake and fed chiefly on boiled periwinkles. And all these seven families lived together in the utmost fun and felicity.

5. How do the author's descriptions of the animals' habitats affect the tone of the story?

Ⓐ They make the animals appear hungry all the time.
Ⓑ They make the animals seem greedy.
Ⓒ They create a tone of nonsense and silliness.
Ⓓ They show how diverse the animals are.

THE WONDERFUL HAIR by A. H. Wraitslaw

Read the story below and answer the questions that follow.

There was a man who was very poor, but so well supplied with children that he was utterly unable to maintain them, and one morning more than once prepared to kill them, in order not to see their misery in dying of hunger, but his wife prevented him. One night a child came to him in his sleep, and said to him: "Man! I see that you are making up your mind to destroy and to kill your poor little children, and I know that you are distressed there at; but in the morning you will find under your pillow a mirror, a red kerchief, and an embroidered pocket-handkerchief; take all three secretly and tell nobody; then go to such a hill; by it, you will find a stream; go along it

till you come to its fountain-head; there you will find a damsel as bright as the sun, with her hair hanging down over her back. Be on your guard, that the ferocious she-dragon do not coil round you; do not converse with her if she speaks; for if you converse with her, she will poison you, and turn you into a fish or something else, and will then devour you but if she bids you examine her head, examine it, and as you turn over her hair, look, and you will find one hair as red as blood; pull it out and run back again; then, if she suspects and begins to run after you, throw her first the embroidered pocket-handkerchief, then the kerchief, and, lastly, the mirror; then she will find occupation for herself. And sell that hair to some rich man, but don't let them cheat you, for that hair is worth countless wealth;

and you will thus enrich yourself and maintain your children."

When the poor man awoke, he found everything under his pillow, just as the child had told him in his sleep; and then he went to the hill. When there, he found the stream, went on and on alongside of it, till he came to the fountain-head. Having looked about him to see where the damsel was, he espied her above a piece of water, like sunbeams threaded on a needle, and she was embroidering at a frame on stuff, the threads of which were young men's hair. As soon as he saw her, he made a reverence to her, and she stood on her feet and questioned him: "Whence are you, unknown young man?" But he held his tongue. She questioned him again: "Who are you? Why have you come?" and much else of all sorts, but he was as mute as a stone, making signs with his hands as if he were deaf and wanted help. Then she told him to sit down on her skirt. He did not wait for any more orders but sat down, and she bent down her head to him, that he might examine it. Turning over the hair of her head, as if to examine it, he was not long in finding that red hair, and separated it from the other hair, pulled it out, jumped off her skirt, and ran away back as he best could. She noticed it and ran at his heels full speed after him. He looked round, and seeing that she was about to overtake him, threw, as he was told, the embroidered pocket-handkerchief on the way, and when she saw the pocket-handkerchief, she stooped and began to overhaul it in every direction, admiring the embroidery, till he had got a good way off. Then the damsel placed the pocket-handkerchief in her bosom and ran after him again. When he saw that she was about to overtake him, he threw the red kerchief, and she again occupied herself, admiring and gazing, till the poor man had again got a good way off. Then the damsel became exasperated, and threw both the pocket-handkerchief and the kerchief on the way, and ran after him in pursuit. Again, when he saw that she was about to overtake him, he threw the mirror. When the damsel came to the mirror, the like of which she had never seen before, she lifted it up, and when she saw herself in it, not knowing that it was herself, but thinking that it was somebody else, she, as it were, fell in love with herself in the mirror, and the man got so far off that she was no longer able to overtake him. When she saw that she could not catch him, she turned back, and the man reached his home safe and sound. After arriving at his home, he showed his wife the hair and told her all that had happened to him, but she began to jeer and laugh at him. But he paid no attention to her and went to a town to sell the hair. A crowd of all sorts of people and merchants collected round him; one offered a sequin, another two, and so on, higher and higher, till they came to a hundred gold sequins. Just then, the emperor heard of the hair, summoned the man into his presence, and said to him that he would give him a thousand sequins for it, and he sold it to him. What was the hair? The emperor split it in two from top to bottom and found registered in it in writing many remarkable things, which happened in the olden time since the beginning of the world. Thus the man became rich and lived on with his wife and children. And that child, that came to him in his sleep was an angel sent by the Lord God, whose will it was to aid the poor man and to reveal secrets which had not been revealed till then.

6. What is the tone at the end of this story?

Ⓐ Serious
Ⓑ Joyful
Ⓒ Angry
Ⓓ Confused

"Base Details"
by Siegfried Sassoon

Read the poem below and answer the questions that follow.

IF I were fierce, and bald, and short of breath,
I'd live with scarlet Majors at the Base,
And speed glum heroes up the line to death.

You'd see me with my puffy petulant face,
Guzzling and gulping in the best hotel,
Reading the Roll of Honour. 'Poor young chap,'
I'd say—'I used to know his father well;
Yes, we've lost heavily in this last scrap.'

And when the war is done and youth stone dead,
I'd toddle safely home and die—in bed.

7. What is the narrator's tone toward the officers at the base?

Ⓐ He respects the decisions they make about the war.
Ⓑ He looks forward to moving up the ranks and becoming an officer.
Ⓒ He is an officer and feels his decisions are well-thought out.
Ⓓ He believes the officers are fat and greedy and don't value the young soldiers.

O Captain! My Captain! By Walt Whitman

Read the poem below and answer the questions that follow.

O Captain! my Captain! our fearful trip is done,
The ship has weather'd every rack, the prize we sought is won,
The port is near, the bells I hear, the people all exulting,
While follow eyes the steady keel, the vessel grim and daring;

But O heart! heart! heart!
O the bleeding drops of red,
Where on the deck my Captain lies,
Fallen cold and dead.

O Captain! my Captain! rise up and hear the bells;
Rise up--for you the flag is flung--for you the bugle trills,
For you bouquets and ribbon'd wreaths--for you the shores a-crowding,
For you they call, the swaying mass, their eager faces turning;
Here Captain! dear father!
This arm beneath your head!
It is some dream that on the deck,
You've fallen cold and dead.

My Captain does not answer, his lips are pale and still,
My father does not feel my arm, he has no pulse nor will,
The ship is anchor'd safe and sound, its voyage closed and done,
From fearful trip the victor ship comes in with object won;
Exult O shores, and ring O bells!
But I with mournful tread,
Walk the deck my Captain lies,
Fallen cold and dead.

8. Complete the following lines based on the poem?

_____ Oh shores!

The prize we _____ is won

While follow eyes the steady_____.

Its _____ closed and done.

But I with _____ tread.

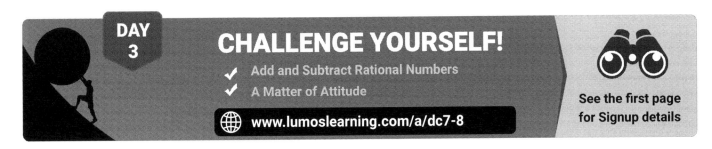

1. Which of the following is the same as 7 − (3 + 4)?

   Ⓐ 7 + (−3) + (−4)
   Ⓑ 7 +(−3 + 4)
   Ⓒ 7 + 7
   Ⓓ −7 − 7

2. Which of the following expressions represents the distance between the two points?

   Ⓐ |4-3|
   Ⓑ (-3)-4
   Ⓒ |(-3)-4|
   Ⓓ 4-3

3. Kyle and Mark started at the same location. Kyle traveled 5 miles due east, while Mark traveled 3 miles due West. How far apart are they?

   Ⓐ 2 miles
   Ⓑ 8 miles
   Ⓒ 15 miles
   Ⓓ 12 miles

4. State whether a number and its inverse are added in these expressions. If yes, select additive inverse is added. If no, select additive inverse is not added.

	Additive Inverse is added	Additive Inverse is not added
3 + (-3)	○	○
-2.2 + 2.2	○	○
1 + 1	○	○
$-\frac{4}{7} + \left(-\frac{4}{7}\right)$	○	○

"Do Not Go Gentle into that Good Night"
Dylan Thomas

Read the poem below and answer the questions that follow.

Do not go gentle into that good night,
Old age should burn and rave at close of day;
Rage, rage against the dying of the light.
Though wise men at their end know dark is right,
Because their words had forked no lightning they
Do not go gentle into that good night.
Good men, the last wave by, crying how bright
Their frail deeds might have danced in a green bay,
Rage, rage against the dying of the light.
Wild men who caught and sang the sun in flight,
And learn, too late, they grieved it on its way,
Do not go gentle into that good night.
Grave men, near death, who see with blinding sight
Blind eyes could blaze like meteors and be gay,
Rage, rage against the dying of the light.
And you, my father, there on the sad height,
Curse, bless me now with your fierce tears, I pray.
Do not go gentle into that good night.
Rage, rage against the dying of the light.

5. Which characteristic of this poem indicates it is a villanelle?

Ⓐ There are two rhyming patterns.
Ⓑ The poem is written in iambic meter.
Ⓒ The subject of the poem is death.
Ⓓ There is a chorus or refrain between every two stanzas.

6. Which answer does not use repetition to develop the tone of this poem?

Ⓐ The word rage is repeated to develop the idea that one can fight back against death.
Ⓑ The word men is repeated to remind the subject about whom he is writing.
Ⓒ The word gentle is repeated to remind the reader how to behave.
Ⓓ The word me is repeated to establish the focus of the poem.

7. How is end rhyme used to make connections between the stanzas?

Ⓐ Every other line rhymes.
Ⓑ Each stanza uses the same rhyme scheme.
Ⓒ The rhyme scheme changes every other stanza.
Ⓓ The last line of each stanza rhymes with the first line of the next stanza.

Landing of the Pilgrims
-by Felicia D. Hemans , public domain

Read the poem below and answer the questions that follow.

The breaking waves dashed high
On a stern and rock-bound coast,
And the woods against a stormy sky
Their giant branches tossed;

And the heavy night hung dark
The hills and waters o'er,
When a band of exiles moored their bark
On the wild New England shore

Not as the conqueror comes,
They, the truehearted, came;
Not with the roll of the stirring drums
And the trumpet that sings of fame;

Not as the flying come,
In silence and in fear,
They shook the depths of the desert gloom
With their hymns of lofty cheer

What sought they thus afar?
Bright jewels of the mine?
The wealth of seas, the spoils of war?
They sought a faith's pure shrine!

Ay, call it holy ground –
The soil where they first trod;
They have left unstained what there they found:
Freedom to worship God!

8. What is described in the second stanza of the poem? Write your answer in the box below.

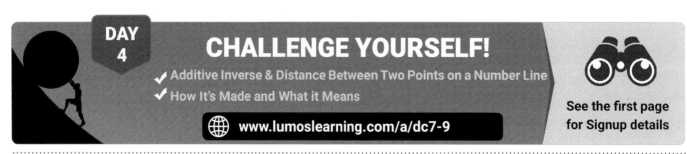

1. **What property is illustrated in the equation?:**

$$7 + \frac{1}{2} = \frac{1}{2} + 7$$

- Ⓐ Commutative property of addition
- Ⓑ Associate property of addition
- Ⓒ Distributive property
- Ⓓ Identity property of addition

2. **Which is a valid use of properties to make the expression easier to calculate?**

$$92 - 8 = ?$$

- Ⓐ $90 - 2 - 8$
- Ⓑ $82 - (10 - 8)$
- Ⓒ $82 + (10 - 8)$
- Ⓓ $(80 + 2) - 8$

3. **Find the sum of the mixed numbers.**

$$4\frac{7}{8} + 7\frac{5}{8}$$

- Ⓐ $11\frac{5}{8}$
- Ⓑ $12\frac{1}{2}$
- Ⓒ $12\frac{7}{8}$
- Ⓓ $11\frac{1}{2}$

4. **Write the correct absolute value expression or distance description into the blanks in the table.**

Distance between 4 and -1	$\lvert-1-4\rvert$	$\lvert 4-(-1)\rvert$
Distance between -4 and -1		$\lvert-4-(-1)\rvert$
Distance between 4 and 1	$\lvert 1-4\rvert$	
	$\lvert 1-(-4)\rvert$	$\lvert-4-1\rvert$

THE EMPEROR'S NEW CLOTHES
by: Hans Christian Anderson

Read the story below and answer the questions that follow.

Many years ago there was an Emperor, who was so excessively fond of new clothes that he spent all his money on them. He cared nothing about his soldiers, nor for the theatre, nor for driving in the woods except for the sake of showing off his new clothes. He had a costume for every hour in the day, and instead of saying, as one does about any other king or emperor, 'He is in his council chamber,' here one always said, 'The Emperor is in his dressing-room.'

Life was very gay in the great town where he lived; hosts of strangers came to visit it every day and among them one day two swindlers. They gave themselves out as weavers and said that they knew how to weave the most beautiful stuff imaginable. Not only were the colors and patterns unusually fine, but the clothes that were made of the stuff had the peculiar quality of becoming invisible to every person who was not fit for the office he held, or if he was impossibly dull.

Those must be splendid clothes,' thought the Emperor. 'By wearing them, I should be able to discover which men in my kingdom are unfitted for their posts. I shall distinguish the wise men from the fools. Yes, I certainly must order some of that stuff to be woven for me.

He paid the two swindlers a lot of money in advance so that they might begin their work at once.

They did put up two looms and pretended to weave, but they had nothing whatever upon their shuttles. At the outset, they asked for a quantity of the finest silk and the purest gold thread, all of which they put into their own bags while they worked away at the empty looms far into the night. I should like to know how those weavers are getting on with the stuff,' thought the Emperor; but he felt a little queer when he reflected that anyone who was stupid or unfit for his post would not be able to see it. He certainly thought that he need have no fears for himself, but still, he thought he would send somebody else first to see how it was getting on. Everybody in the town knew what wonderful power the stuff possessed, and everyone was anxious to see how stupid his neighbor was.

I will send my faithful old minister to the weavers,' thought the Emperor. 'He will be best able to see how the stuff looks, for he is a clever man, and no one fulfills his duties better than he does!'

So the good old minister went into the room where the two swindlers sat working at the empty loom.

Heaven preserve us!' thought the old minister, opening his eyes very wide. 'Why, I can't see a thing!' But he took care not to say so.
Both the swindlers begged him to be good enough to step a little nearer and asked if he did not think it a good pattern and beautiful coloring. They pointed to the empty loom, and the poor old minister stared as hard as he could, but he could not see anything, for of course there was nothing to see. Good heavens!' thought he, 'is it possible that I am a fool. I have never thought so, and nobody must know it. Am I not fit for my post? It will never

do to say that I cannot see the stuff.

Well, sir, you don't say anything about the stuff,' said the one who was pretending to weave. Oh, it is beautiful! quite charming!' said the old minister, looking through his spectacles; 'this pattern and these colors! I will certainly tell the Emperor that the stuff pleases me very much.

We are delighted to hear you say so,' said the swindlers, and then they named all the colors and described the peculiar pattern. The old minister paid great attention to what they said, so as to be able to repeat it when he got home to the Emperor.

Then the swindlers went on to demand more money, more silk, and more gold, to be able to proceed with the weaving; but they put it all into their own pockets—not a single strand was ever put into the loom, but they went on as before weaving at the empty loom.

The Emperor soon sent another faithful official to see how the stuff was getting on, and if it would soon be ready. The same thing happened to him as to the minister; he looked and looked, but as there was only the empty loom, he could see nothing at all.

Is not this a beautiful piece of stuff?' said both the swindlers, showing and explaining the beautiful pattern and colors which were not there to be seen.

I know I am not a fool!' thought the man, 'so it must be that I am unfit for my good post! It is very strange, though! However, one must not let it appear!' So he praised the stuff he did not see and assured them of his delight in the beautiful colors and the originality of the design. 'It is absolutely charming!' he said to the Emperor. Everybody in the town was talking about this splendid stuff.

Now the Emperor thought he would like to see it while it was still on the loom. So, accompanied by a number of selected courtiers, among whom were the two faithful officials who had already seen the imaginary stuff, he went to visit the crafty impostors, who were working away as hard as ever they could at the empty loom.

It is magnificent!' said both the honest officials. 'Only see, your Majesty, what a design! What colors!' And they pointed to the empty loom, for they thought no doubt the others could see the stuff.

What!' thought the Emperor; 'I see nothing at all! This is terrible! Am I a fool? Am I not fit to be Emperor? Why, nothing worse could happen to me!

Oh, it is beautiful!' said the Emperor. 'It has my highest approval!' and he nodded his satisfaction as he gazed at the empty loom. Nothing would induce him to say that he could not see anything.

The whole suite gazed and gazed, but saw nothing more than all the others. However, they all exclaimed with his Majesty, 'It is very beautiful!' and they advised him to wear a suit made of this wonderful cloth on the occasion of a great procession which was just about to take place. 'It is magnificent!
gorgeous! excellent!' went from mouth to mouth; they were all equally delighted with it.

The Emperor gave each of the rogues an order of knighthood to be worn in their buttonholes and the title of 'Gentlemen weavers.'

The swindlers sat up the whole night before the day on which the procession was to take place, burning sixteen candles; so that people might see how anxious they were to get the Emperor's new clothes ready. They pretended to take the stuff off the loom. They cut it out in the air with a huge pair of scissors, and they stitched away with needles without any thread in them. At last, they said: 'Now the Emperor's new clothes are ready!

The Emperor, with his grandest courtiers, went to them himself, and both the swindlers raised one arm in the air, as if they were holding something, and said: 'See, these are the trousers, this is the coat, here is the mantle!' and so on. 'It is as light as a spider's web. One might think one had nothing on, but that is the very beauty of it!'

Yes!' said all the courtiers, but they could not see anything, for there was nothing to see.

Will your imperial majesty be graciously pleased to take off your clothes,' said the impostors, 'so that we may put on the new ones, along here before the great mirror?'

The Emperor took off all his clothes, and the impostors pretended to give him one article of dress after the other of the new ones which they had pretended to make. They pretended to fasten something round his waist and to tie on something; this was the train, and the Emperor turned round and round in front of the mirror.

How well his majesty looks in the new clothes! How becoming they are!' cried all the people around. 'What a design, and what colors! They are the most gorgeous robes!'

The canopy is waiting outside, which is to be carried over your majesty in the procession,' said the master of the ceremonies.

Well, I am quite ready,' said the Emperor. 'Don't the clothes fit well?' and then he turned around again in front of the mirror so that he should seem to be looking at his grand things.

The chamberlains who were to carry the train stooped and pretended to lift it from the ground with both hands, and they walked along with their hands in the air. They dared not let it appear that they could not see anything.

Then the Emperor walked along in the procession under the gorgeous canopy, and everybody in the streets and at the windows exclaimed, 'How beautiful the Emperor's new clothes are! What a splendid train! And they fit to perfection!' Nobody would let it appear that he could see nothing, for then he would not be fit for his post, or else he was a fool.

None of the Emperor's clothes had been so successful before.

But he has got nothing on,' said a little child.

Oh, listen to the innocent,' said its father; and one person whispered to the other what the child had said. 'He has nothing on; a child says he has nothing on!

But he has nothing on!' at last cried all the people.

The Emperor writhed, for he knew it was true, but he thought 'the procession must go on now,' so held himself stiffer than ever, and the chamberlains held up the invisible train.

5. **Which excerpt from the text provides the reason the Emperor agreed to buy clothes from the swindlers?**

Ⓐ Not only were the colors and patterns unusually fine, but the clothes that were made of the stuff had the peculiar quality of becoming invisible to every person who was not fit for the office he held, or if he was impossibly dull.

Ⓑ Life was very gay in the great town where he lived; hosts of strangers came to visit it every day, and among them one day two swindlers. They gave themselves out as weavers, and said that they knew how to weave the most beautiful stuffs imagin able.

Ⓒ At the outset they asked for a quantity of the finest silk and the purest gold thread, all of which they put into their own bags, while they worked away at the empty looms far into the night.

Ⓓ 'I know I am not a fool!' thought the man, 'so it must be that I am unfit for my good post! It is very strange, though! However, one must not let it appear!' So he praised the stuff he did not see, and assured them of his delight in the beautiful colors and the originality of the design.

6. What character trait do the Emperor and his minister share?

Ⓐ They are both insecure about their qualifications.
Ⓑ They both want to fool the public
Ⓒ They both want the Emperor to have the most wonderful clothing available.
Ⓓ Both men are able to imagine things that are not visible.

7. Why does the Emperor continue with the procession after the child reviews the truth?

Ⓐ He doesn't believe the child.
Ⓑ He doesn't want to admit to his subjects that the swindlers had tricked him.
Ⓒ He is concerned that there are people in the audience who can see the clothes.
Ⓓ He has paid for his new clothes and wants to continue showing them off.

O Captain! My Captain! By Walt Whitman

Read the poem below and answer the questions that follow.

O Captain! my Captain! our fearful trip is done,
The ship has weather'd every rack, the prize we sought is won,
The port is near, the bells I hear, the people all exulting,
While follow eyes the steady keel, the vessel grim and daring;

But O heart! heart! heart!
O the bleeding drops of red,
Where on the deck my Captain lies,
Fallen cold and dead.

O Captain! my Captain! rise up and hear the bells;
Rise up--for you the flag is flung--for you the bugle trills,
For you bouquets and ribbon'd wreaths--for you the shores a-crowding,
For you they call, the swaying mass, their eager faces turning;
Here Captain! dear father!
This arm beneath your head!
It is some dream that on the deck,
You've fallen cold and dead.

My Captain does not answer, his lips are pale and still,
My father does not feel my arm, he has no pulse nor will,
The ship is anchor'd safe and sound, its voyage closed and done,
From fearful trip the victor ship comes in with object won;
Exult O shores, and ring O bells!
But I with mournful tread,
Walk the deck my Captain lies,
Fallen cold and dead.

8. **Tell how the vocabulary in this poem helps you to visualize the scene. Write your answer in the box below.**

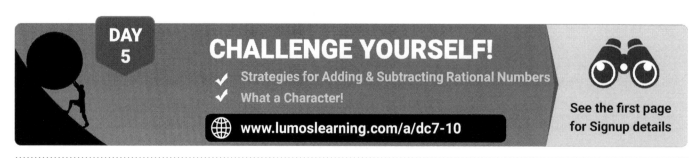

6 WAYS TO BECOME A WAKE BOARD WHIZ

1.   Relax and be Patient

Relaxing on the board helps you get a better center of gravity, which keeps you stable on the board. The more loose and relaxed you are, the better balance you will have. Bend your knees, stay low to the board, keep your arms straight and let the boat pull you. Focus on staying balanced first; you can try the fancy tricks when you get more comfortable on the board.

2.   Know Which Foot Goes First

Once you're up on the board, figure out which foot you want to be forward. The two ways you can position your feet are "regular" and "goofy." The "regular" position is when the left foot is forward on the board, and "goofy" is when the right foot leads. Don't let the names of the positions sway you to choose a certain way; both stances are totally normal; just choose to lead with whichever foot is more comfortable and feels natural.

3.   Control your Board

Once you are totally comfortable standing on the board, you can practice controlling the board. Controlling the board allows you to decide which way you are going and lays the foundation for future, more complicated, tricks. To control the board, you want to lean away from the boat, shift your weight to your heels, and "carve" through the water by transferring your weight to your toes and back again.

4.   Practice on Land

Thankfully, there are many ways to practice your wakeboard skills during the colder seasons that don't involve getting into freezing water. While on land, you can practice different balance exercises, like yoga, or you could invest in a balance board. A balance board is a board with a wheel in the middle that can be used indoors. To use it, you put your foot on either side of the board and try to stay stable to improve your balance. Once you get better at balance, you can also try doing tricks on your balance board. This type of board improves your balance and strengthens your ankles, which will help you significantly once it's time to get back in the water. You can also practice on land through skateboarding or snowboarding. Both use similar muscles and can help you practice your balance, which lets you practice your skills on the offseason.

5.   Lift More Weights

You might not think that lifting weights and getting stronger would help your wakeboarding skills, but it does. Wakeboarding uses so many muscles that you don't even think about- Biceps, abdominals, back, legs, forearms, etc. It truly is a sport that exercises the whole body, which is why it is important to strength train. Having strong muscles helps your balance on the board, your ability to do tricks, and allows you to get better faster than someone who does not weight train. Strength training also helps prevent injuries, as the stronger you are, the easier it will be to ride with the correct form.

6.   Try some Tricks

Once you have the basics down, you can start practicing tricks. One of the most basic tricks is Ollie. An ollie is simply a jump that you do while on the board. To do an ollie, get up on the board and begin riding. Once you feel comfortable on the board, shift your weight to your back leg and lift your front leg quickly, pushing off from the water from the back of the board. Once you're in the air, bring your back leg up to the same level as your front leg to level the board. When landing, try to keep the board flat, putting equal pressure on both of your feet. This keeps your board from braking and you from falling off. Once you perfect the ollie, you can start doing more complicated tricks.

WEEK 3
SUMMER PRACTICE

DAY 1

1. **Fill in the blank to make a true equation.**

   (-9)*(___) = 36

   Ⓐ - 4
   Ⓑ   4
   Ⓒ   6
   Ⓓ - 6

2. **Simplify the following complex fraction.**

   $$\frac{\dfrac{1}{2}}{\dfrac{2}{3}}$$

   Ⓐ $\dfrac{4}{3}$

   Ⓑ $\dfrac{1}{2}$

   Ⓒ $\dfrac{3}{4}$

   Ⓓ $\dfrac{4}{3}$

3. **Fill in the table with correct multiplication expression for each division expression or the correct division expression for each multiplication expression.**

Division Expression	Multiplication Expression
$\dfrac{\frac{-1}{3}}{\frac{7}{8}}$	$\dfrac{-1}{3} \times \dfrac{8}{7}$
$\dfrac{\frac{4}{3}}{-5}$	
$\dfrac{-6}{\frac{8}{9}}$	$-6 \times \dfrac{9}{8}$
	$\dfrac{-7}{3} \times \dfrac{9}{4}$
$\dfrac{\frac{-6}{11}}{\frac{-4}{5}}$	

4. **Solve for x.**

$x = (-2)(6)(-4)$

- Ⓐ x = 36
- Ⓑ x = 0
- Ⓒ x = 48
- Ⓓ x = - 48

"The Smith and the Fairies": A Gaelic Folk Tale (Ed. Kate Douglas Wiggin)

Read the story below and answer the questions that follow.

Years ago, there lived in Crossbrig, a smith of the name of MacEachern. This man had an only child, a boy of about thirteen or fourteen years of age, cheerful, strong, and healthy. All of a sudden, he fell ill, took to his bed, and moped whole days away. No one could tell what was the matter with him, and the boy himself could not, or would not, tell how he felt. He was wasting away fast; getting thin, old, and yellow; and his father and all his friends were afraid that he would die.

At last one day, after the boy had been lying in this condition for a long time, getting neither better nor worse, always confined to bed, but with an extraordinary appetite—one day, while sadly revolving these things, and standing idly at his forge, with no heart to work, the smith was agreeably surprised to see an old man, well known for his sagacity and knowledge of out-of-the-way things, walk into his workshop. Forthwith he told him the occurrence which had clouded his life.

The old man looked grave as he listened, and after sitting a long time pondering over all he had heard, gave his opinion thus: "It is not your son you have got. The boy has been carried away by the 'Daione Sith,' and they have left a Sibhreach in his place".

"Alas! and what then am I to do?" said the smith. "How am I ever to see my own son again?"

"I will tell you how," answered the old man. "But, first, to make sure that it is not your own son you have got, take as many empty egg-shells as you can get, go into his room, spread them out carefully before his sight, then proceed to draw water with them, carrying them two and two in your hands as if they were a great weight, and arrange them when full, with every sort of earnestness around the fire." The smith accordingly gathered as many broken egg-shells as he could get, went into the room, and proceeded to carry out all his instructions.

He had not been long at work before there arose from the bed a shout of laughter, and the voice of the seeming sick boy exclaimed, "I am eight hundred years of age, and I have never seen the like of that before." The smith returned and told the old man.

"Well, now," said the sage to him, "did I not tell you that it was not your son you had: your son is in Borracheill in a digh there (that is, a round green hill frequented by fairies). Get rid as soon as possible of this intruder, and I think I may promise you your son. You must light a very large and bright fire before the bed on which this stranger is lying. He will ask you, 'What is the use of such a fire as that?' Answer him at once, 'You will see that presently!' and then seize him and throw him into the middle of it. If it is your own son you have got, he will call out to you to save him; but if not, the thing will fly through the roof".

The smith again followed the old man's advice: kindled a large fire, answered the question put to him as he had been directed to do, and seizing the child flung him in without hesitation. The Sibhreach gave an awful yell and sprang through the roof, where a hole had been left to let the smoke out.

On a certain night, the old man told him the green round hill, where the fairies kept the boy, would be open, and on that date the smith, having provided himself with a Bible, a dirk, and a crowing cock, was to proceed to the hill. He would hear singing and dancing, and much merriment going on, he had been told, but he was to advance boldly; the Bible he carried would be a certain safeguard to him against any danger from the fairies. On entering the hill he was to stick the dirk in the threshold, to prevent the hill from closing upon him; "and then," continued the old man, "on entering you will see a spacious apartment before you, beautifully clean, and there, standing far within, working at a forge, you will also see your own son. When you are questioned, say you come to seek him, and will not go without him".

Not long after this, the time came round, and the smith sallied forth, prepared as instructed. Sure enough, as he approached the hill, there was a light where the light was seldom seen before. Soon after, a sound of piping, dancing, and joyous merriment reached the anxious father on the night wind.

Overcoming every impulse to fear, the smith approached the threshold steadily, stuck the dirk into it as directed, and entered. Protected by the Bible he carried on his breast, the fairies could not touch him; but they asked him, with a good deal of displeasure, what he wanted there. He answered, "I want my son, whom I see down there, and I will not go without him."

Upon hearing this, the whole company before him gave a loud laugh, which wakened up the cock he carried dozing in his arms, who at once leaped upon his shoulders, clapped his wings lustily, and crowed loud and long.

The fairies, incensed, seized the smith and his son and throwing them out of the hill, flung the dirk after them, and in an instant, all was dark.

For a year and a day the boy never did a turn of work, and hardly ever spoke a word; but at last one day, sitting by his father and watching him finishing a sword he was making for some chief, and which he was very particular about, he suddenly exclaimed, "That is not the way to do it;" and taking the tools from his father's hands he set to work himself in his place, and soon fashioned a sword, the like of which was never seen in the country before.

From that day the young man wrought constantly with his father and became the inventor of a
peculiarly fine and well-tempered weapon, the making of which kept the two Smiths, father and son, in constant employment, spread their fame far and wide, and gave them the means in abundance, as they before had the disposition, to live content with all the world and very happy with each other.

5. How is the fairy pretend version of the smith's son different than the smith's actual son?

Ⓐ The fairy is a humorous trickster, while the real son is quiet and serious.
Ⓑ The fairy is cruel to the father, while the real son is kind to his father.
Ⓒ The fairy and the son are exactly alike.
Ⓓ The fairy and the father are alike.

Read the story below and answer the questions that follow.

An honest and poor old woman was washing clothes at a pool when a bird that a hunter had disabled by a shot in the wing fell down into the water before her. She gently took up the bird, carried it home with her, dressed its wound, and fed it until it was well when it soared away. Some days later, it returned, put before her an oval seed, and departed again. The woman planted the seed in her yard, and when it came up, she recognized the leaf as that of a melon. She made a trellis for it, and gradually a fruit formed on it, and grew to great size.

Toward the end of the year, the old dame was unable to pay her debts, and her poverty so weighed upon her that she became ill. Sitting one day at her door, feverish and tired, she saw that the melon was ripe and looked luscious, so she determined to try its unknown quality. Taking a knife, she severed the melon from its stalk and was surprised to hear it chink in her hands. On cutting it in two, she found it full of silver and gold pieces, with which she paid her debts and bought supplies for many days.

Among her neighbors was a busybody who craftily found out how the old woman had so suddenly become rich. Thinking there was no good reason why she should not herself be equally fortunate, she washed clothes at the pool, keeping a sharp lookout for birds until she managed to hit and maim one of a flock that was flitting over the water. She then took the disabled bird home and treated it with care until its wing healed, and it flew away. Shortly afterward, it came back with a seed in its beak, laid it before her, and again took flight. The woman quickly planted the seed, saw it come up and spread its leaves, made a trellis for it, and had the gratification of seeing a melon form on its stalk. In the prospect of her future wealth, she ate rich food, bought fine garments, and got so deeply into debt that, before the end of the year, she was harried by duns. But the melon grew apace, and she was delighted to find that, as it ripened, it became of vast size and that when she shook it, there was a great rattling inside. At the end of the year, she cut it down, and divided it, expecting it to be a coffer of coins; but there crawled out of it two old, lame, hungry beggars, who told her they would remain and eat at her table as long as they lived.

6. How are the busybody neighbor and the honest old woman different?

Ⓐ They are not different. They are both poor and hungry.
Ⓑ The honest old woman acts out of selflessness while the busybody neighbor acts out of self-interest.
Ⓒ The honest old woman is much poorer than the busybody neighbor.
Ⓓ The honest old woman minds her own business while the busybody neighbor is concerned with everyone else's business.

7. How would this story be different if the busybody neighbor was the first to receive a melon seed?

Ⓐ She would have gotten a garden full of melons to eat and the old, honest woman would be left with a garden full of beggars.
Ⓑ Both the busybody neighbor and the old, honest woman would no longer be poor.
Ⓒ There would be no difference. The busybody neighbor would have still gotten a garden of beggars because of the way she went about getting her melon seed.
Ⓓ The busybody would tell everyone about the melon.

Excerpt from The Wonderful Wizard of Oz
L. Frank Baum

Read the story below and answer the questions that follow.

Dorothy lived in the midst of the great Kansas prairies, with Uncle Henry, who was a farmer, and Aunt Em, who was the farmer's wife. Their house was small, for the lumber to build it had to be carried by wagon many miles. There were four walls, a floor and a roof, which made one room; and this room contained a rusty looking cooking stove, a cupboard for the dishes, a table, three or four chairs, and the beds. Uncle Henry and Aunt Em had a big bed in one corner, and Dorothy a little bed in another corner. There was no garret at all, and no cellar-except a small hole dug in the ground, called a cyclone cellar, where the family could go in case one of those great whirlwinds arose, mighty enough to crush any building in its path. It was reached by a trapdoor in the middle of the floor, from which a ladder led down into the small, dark hole.

When Dorothy stood in the doorway and looked around, she could see nothing but the great gray prairie on every side. Not a tree nor a house broke the broad sweep of flat country that reached the edge of the sky in all directions. The sun had baked the plowed land into a gray mass, with little cracks running through it. Even the grass was not green, for the sun had burned the tops of the long blades until they were the same gray color to be seen everywhere. Once the house had been painted, but the sun blistered the paint, and the rains washed it away, and now the house was as dull and gray as everything else.

When Aunt Em came there to live, she was a young, pretty wife. The sun and wind had changed her, too. They had taken the sparkle from her eyes and left them a sober gray; they had taken the red from her cheeks and lips, and they were gray also. She was thin and gaunt and never smiled now. When Dorothy, who was an orphan, first came to her, Aunt Em had been so startled by the child's laughter that she would scream and press her hand upon her heart whenever Dorothy's merry voice reached her ears; and she still looked at the little girl with wonder that she could find anything to laugh at.

Uncle Henry never laughed. He worked hard from morning till night and did not know what joy was. He was gray also, from his long beard to his rough boots, and he looked stern and solemn, and rarely spoke.

It was Toto that made Dorothy laugh, and saved her from growing as gray as her other surroundings. Toto was not gray; he was a little black dog, with long, silky hair and small black eyes that twinkled merrily on either side of his funny, wee nose. Toto played all day long, and Dorothy played with him and loved him dearly.

To-day, however, they were not playing. Uncle Henry sat upon the door-step and looked anxiously at the sky, which was even grayer than usual. Dorothy stood in the door with Toto in her arms and looked at the sky too. Aunt Em was washing the dishes.

From the far north, they heard a low wail of the wind, and Uncle Henry and Dorothy could see where the long grass bowed in waves before the coming storm. There now came a sharp whistling in the air from the south, and as they turned their eyes that way, they saw ripples in the grass coming from that direction also.

Suddenly Uncle Henry stood up.

"There's a cyclone coming, Em," he called to his wife; "I'll go look after the stock." Then he ran toward the sheds where the cows and horses were kept.

Aunt Em dropped her work and came to the door. One glance told her of the danger close at hand.

"Quick, Dorothy!" she screamed, "run for the cellar!"

Toto jumped out of Dorothy's arms and hid under the bed, and the girl started to get him. Aunt Em, badly frightened, threw open the trap-door in the floor and climbed down the ladder into the small, dark hole. Dorothy caught Toto at last and started to follow her aunt. When she was halfway across the room, there came a great shriek from the wind, and the house shook so hard that she lost her footing and sat down suddenly upon the floor.

8. Part A
How is Aunt Em different from how she was when she first married Uncle Henry?

Ⓐ She is more cautious about the weather.
Ⓑ She doesn't smile as often as she used to.
Ⓒ She no longer enjoys the company of children.
Ⓓ She wears only gray clothing.

Part B
What behavior of Dorothy's did Aunt Em find almost frightening?

Ⓐ Dorothy's laughter.
Ⓑ Dorothy's love for her dog, Toto.
Ⓒ Dorothy's lack of caution during a storm.
Ⓓ Dorothy's laziness.

DAY 1

CHALLENGE YOURSELF!
✔ Rational Numbers, Multiplication and Division
✔ Finding Patterns – Comparing and Contrasting

🌐 www.lumoslearning.com/a/dc7-11

See the first page for Signup details

1. **Which of the following division problems CANNOT be completed?**

   Ⓐ $10 \div 0$
   Ⓑ $155 \div (-3)$
   Ⓒ $(2/3) \div (1/4)$
   Ⓓ $0 \div 5$

2. **Kathy is laying stepping stones in her garden. The stones are 8 inches long, and she wants to create a path that is 10 feet long. How many stones will she need?**

   Ⓐ 10 stones
   Ⓑ 80 stones
   Ⓒ 15 stones
   Ⓓ 1.25 stones

3. **Jared hiked a trail that is 12 miles long. He hiked the trail in section that were 1.5 miles each. In how many sections did he complete the hike?**

   Ⓐ 12
   Ⓑ 10
   Ⓒ 8
   Ⓓ 6

4. **Complete the fraction:** $\dfrac{?}{3} = -5$ **. Write your answer in the box given below.**

"Paul Revere's Ride" (Excerpt)
Henry Wadsworth Longfellow

Read the poem below and answer the questions that follow.

Listen my children and you shall hear
Of the midnight ride of Paul Revere,
On the eighteenth of April, in Seventy-five;
Hardly a man is now alive
Who remembers that famous day and year.
He said to his friend, "If the British march
By land or sea from the town to-night,
Hang a lantern aloft in the belfry arch
Of the North Church tower as a signal light,--
One if by land, and two if by sea;
And I on the opposite shore will be,
Ready to ride and spread the alarm
Through every Middlesex village and farm,
For the country folk to be up and to arm."
Then he said "Good-night!" and with muffled oar
Silently rowed to the Charlestown shore,
Just as the moon rose over the bay,
Where swinging wide at her moorings lay
The Somerset, British man-of-war;
A phantom ship, with each mast and spar
Across the moon like a prison bar,
And a huge black hulk, that was magnified
By its own reflection in the tide.

It was twelve by the village clock
When he crossed the bridge into Medford town.
He heard the crowing of the cock,
And the barking of the farmer's dog,
And felt the damp of the river fog,
That rises after the sun goes down.
It was one by the village clock,
When he galloped into Lexington.
He saw the gilded weathercock

Swim in the moonlight as he passed,
And the meeting-house windows, black and bare,
Gaze at him with a spectral glare,

As if they already stood aghast
At the bloody work they would look upon.
It was two by the village clock,
When he came to the bridge in Concord town.
He heard the bleating of the flock,

And the twitter of birds among the trees,
And felt the breath of the morning breeze
Blowing over the meadow brown.
And one was safe and asleep in his bed
Who at the bridge would be first to fall,
Who that day would be lying dead,
Pierced by a British musket ball.
You know the rest. In the books you have read
How the British Regulars fired and fled,---
How the farmers gave them ball for ball,
From behind each fence and farmyard wall,
Chasing the redcoats down the lane,
Then crossing the fields to emerge again
Under the trees at the turn of the road,
And only pausing to fire and load.

The Real Story of Revere's Ride

From the Paul Revere House official Website
In 1774 and the Spring of 1775 Paul Revere
was employed by the Boston Committee of
Correspondence and the Massachusetts
Committee of Safety as an express rider to
carry news, messages, and copies of resolu-
tions as far away as New York and Philadel-
phia.

On the evening of April 18, 1775, Paul Revere
was sent for by Dr. Joseph Warren and instructed to ride to Lexington, Massachusetts,
to warn Samuel Adams and John Hancock
that British troops were marching to arrest
them. After being rowed across the Charles
River to Charlestown by two associates, Paul

Revere borrowed a horse from his friend Deacon John Larkin. While in Charlestown, he verified that the local "Sons of Liberty" committee had seen his pre-arranged signals. (Two lanterns had been hung briefly in the bell-tower of Christ Church in Boston, indicating that troops would row "by sea" across the Charles River to Cambridge, rather than marching "by land" out Boston Neck. Revere had arranged for these signals the previous weekend, as he was afraid that he might be prevented from leaving Boston).

On the way to Lexington, Revere "alarmed" the country-side, stopping at each house, and arrived in Lexington about midnight. As he approached the house where Adams and Hancock were staying, a sentry asked that he not make so much noise. "Noise!" cried Revere, "You'll have noise enough before long. The regulars are coming out!" After delivering his message, Revere was joined by a second rider, William Dawes, who had been sent on the same errand by a different route. Deciding on their own to continue on to Concord, Massachusetts, where weapons and supplies were hidden, Revere and Dawes were joined by a third rider, Dr. Samuel Prescott. Soon after, all three were arrested by a British patrol. Prescott escaped almost immediately, and Dawes soon after. Revere was held for some time and then released. Left without a horse, Revere returned to Lexington in time to witness part of the battle on the Lexington Green.

5. According to the poem, what was the purpose of Revere's ride?

- (A) To alert everyone in the county that the British were approaching.
- (B) To warn Samuel Adams and John Hancock that the British were approaching.
- (C) To make it back to Boston in time for the battle.
- (D) To reach Lexington before the British troops to awaken the members of the militia.

6. According to the non-fiction passage, what was the purpose of Revere's ride?

- (A) To alert everyone in the county that the British were approaching.
- (B) To warn Samuel Adams and John Hancock that the British were approaching.
- (C) To make it back to Boston in time for the battle.
- (D) To reach Lexington before the British troops to awaken the members of the militia.

7. What information from the non-fiction passage does the poem exclude?

- (A) The description of the signals in the church steeple.
- (B) That Revere was arrested and held by the British.
- (C) That Revere reached the town of Lexington.
- (D) That the British soldiers were coming by sea.

8. About whom might Longfellow have just as accurately written this poem?

- (A) Samuel Adams
- (B) John Larkin
- (C) Samuel Prescott
- (D) William Dawes

1. **Which of these multiplication expressions is equivalent to the division expression:**

$$-\frac{4}{23} \div \frac{7}{58}$$ **Circle the correct answer choice.**

Ⓐ $-\dfrac{23}{4} \times \dfrac{58}{7}$

Ⓑ $-\dfrac{4}{23} \times \dfrac{58}{7}$

Ⓒ $-\dfrac{23}{4} \times \dfrac{7}{58}$

Ⓓ $-\dfrac{4}{23} \times \dfrac{7}{58}$

2. **Which property is illustrated in the following statement?**

$$(5)(4)(7) = (7)(5)(4)$$

Ⓐ Triple multiplication property
Ⓑ Distributive property
Ⓒ Commutative property of multiplication
Ⓓ Associative property of multiplication

3. **Find the quotient:** $4 \div \dfrac{1}{2}$

Ⓐ 4
Ⓑ 8
Ⓒ 2
Ⓓ 16

4. Fill in the table with the correct reciprocals.

$\dfrac{6}{4}$	$\dfrac{4}{6}$
	$\dfrac{-19}{6}$
$\dfrac{5}{-64}$	
	4

From Guiseppi Verdi by Thomas Trapper

Read the information below and answer the questions that follow.

Whenever the organ man came into the village of Roncole, in Italy (where Verdi was born, October 10, 1813), Verdi could not be kept indoors. But he followed the wonderful organ and the wonderful man who played it, all day long, as happy as he could be.

When Giuseppe was seven years old, his father, though only a poor innkeeper, bought him a spinet, a sort of small piano. So faithfully did the little boy practice that the spinet was soon quite worn out and new jacks, or hammers, had to be made for it. This was done by Stephen Cavaletti, who wrote a message on one of the jacks telling that he made them anew and covered them with leather, and fixed the pedal, doing all for nothing, because the little boy, Giuseppe Verdi, showed such willingness to practice and to learn. Thus the good Stephen thought this was pay enough.

5. Which sentence from the passage best explains how Verdi felt about his first spinet?

Ⓐ "But he followed the wonderful organ and wonderful man who played it all day long, as happy as he could be."
Ⓑ "So faithfully did the little boy practice that the spinet was soon quite worn out and new jacks, or hammers, had to be made for it."
Ⓒ "...because the little boy, Giuseppe Verdi, showed such willingness to practice and to learn."
Ⓓ "Thus the good Stephen thought this was pay enough."

From Guiseppi Verdi by Thomas Trapper

Read the information below and answer the questions that follow.

Skunks are omnivores. They can be found eating nuts, berries, roots, leaves, grasses, and even some types of fungi (mushroom-like plants). For animals, they enjoy dining on rodents such as mice and rats, insects, earthworms, frogs, lizards, toads, and birds. Sometimes when they are unable to find live animals to eat, they become scavengers eating dead animals left behind. When they live close to people's homes, skunks sometimes will even get into trash cans, eating garbage.

When skunks eat, they do not limit themselves to small meals. They like to "pig out" on whatever food they can find. When there is a large amount of food available, skunks get very fat very quickly.

http://en.wikipedia.org/wiki/Skunk

6. If you had to answer the question "Can skunks control their appetites?" which sentence would you use to support your answer?

Ⓐ "They can be found eating nuts, berries, roots, leaves, grasses, and even some types of fungi (mushroom-like plants)."

Ⓑ "For animals, they enjoy dining on rodents such as mice and rats, insects, earth worms, frogs, lizards, toads, and birds."

Ⓒ "When they live close to people's homes, skunks sometimes will even get into trash cans, eating garbage."

Ⓓ "They like to 'pig out' on whatever food they can find. When there is a large amount of food, skunks get fat very quickly."

7. If the author removed the sentence telling you skunks were omnivores, could you still infer that skunks are omnivores?

Ⓐ No, because the author does not tell me what an omnivore is or what it eats.

Ⓑ No, because the author does not provide enough information about the types of food a skunk eats.

Ⓒ Yes, because the author shows that a skunk eats both plants and animals.

Ⓓ Yes, because the author says that skunks are also scavengers.

The Assassination of President Lincoln
April 14, 1865

Read the information below and answer the questions that follow.

Shortly after 10 p.m. on April 14, 1865, actor, John Wilkes Booth entered the presidential box at Ford's Theatre in Washington D.C. and fatally shot President Abraham Lincoln. As Lincoln slumped forward in his seat, Booth leapt onto the stage and escaped through the back door. A doctor in the audience rushed over to examine the paralyzed president. Lincoln was then carried across the street to Petersen's Boarding House, where he died early the next morning.

Lincoln was the first president assassinated in U.S. history. Why did Booth do it? He thought it would aid the South, which had just surrendered to Federal forces. It had nearly the opposite effect, ending Lincoln's plans for a rather generous peace. Booth did not act alone. This "wanted" poster ap-

peared everywhere, offering a reward for the arrest of Booth and his accomplices. The conspirators were all captured, and Booth was shot while trying to escape from Union soldiers.

The whole country grieved the death of President Lincoln. As the nine-car funeral train carried President Lincoln home for burial in Springfield, Illinois, people showed up at train stations all along the way to pay their respects.

"The Assassination of President Lincoln." The Assassination of President Lincoln. N.p., n.d. Web. 15 July 2013.

8. **Which detail in the first sentence helps you infer how Booth was able to get access to the theater?**

    Ⓐ It was 10 p.m.

    Ⓑ He was an actor.

    Ⓒ He was going to the presidential box.

    Ⓓ It was on April 14.

1. **Convert to a decimal:** $\dfrac{7}{8}$

    Ⓐ 0.78
    Ⓑ 0.81
    Ⓒ 0.875
    Ⓓ 0.925

2. **Convert to a decimal:** $\dfrac{5}{6}$

    Ⓐ 0.8333333...
    Ⓑ 0.56
    Ⓒ 0.94
    Ⓓ 0.8

3. **How can you tell that the following number is a rational number?**

   0.251

    Ⓐ It is a rational number because the decimal terminates.
    Ⓑ It is a rational number because there is a value of 0 in the ones place.
    Ⓒ It is a rational number because the sum of the digits is less than 10.
    Ⓓ It is a rational number because it is not a repeating decimal.

4. **In the library, there are 230 fiction books, 120 nonfiction books, and 30 magazines. Write the ratio of magazines to nonfiction books as a decimal in the box given below.**

Fall Leaves
USDA Forest Service

Read the information below and answer the questions that follow.

We almost always think of trees as being green, but there is one time of year when their leaves turn a myriad orange, red, yellow, and brown: the beautiful and chilly days of fall. Those living in the Eastern or Northern United States come to anticipate the change in color starting in September or October every single year. But what causes the leaves to change color, and why?

Just like many animals that hibernate for the winter, trees experience a unique change during the winter months. During summer, for instance, plants use the process of photosynthesis to transform carbon dioxide found in the air into organic compounds like sugars using energy from the sun. During the winter, however, there is less light to go around, and their ability to create food from the photosynthesis process is limited.

What does that have to do with a leaf's color? The substance that allows trees to turn carbon dioxide into food (chlorophyll) is also the cause of the leaf's green sheen. As the photosynthesis process wanes in the colder months due to the lack of sun, so does its greenish hue, allowing other elements present in the leaf to show through. Believe it or not, the yellows and oranges that appear in fall have actually been there all year in the form of nutrients like carotene (also found in carrots). The intense green color of the chlorophyll had simply overshadowed them. But what about the reds and browns? And what causes the leaves to fall away after they change color?

The bright reds and purples in each leaf come from a strong antioxidant that many trees create on their own because of their protective qualities. The antioxidant helps protect the trees from the sun, lower their freezing levels, and protect them from frost. As winter comes, so does the need for the antioxidant (similar to the way a dog gets more fur during winter to stay warmer).

As for the leaves falling, that is another story. At the base of each leaf, there is a layer of cells that carry food and water from the leaf to the tree during the summer months to keep it fed. In the fall, that layer actually starts to harden, preventing the passage of nutrients. Because of this, the nutrients and waste that previously passed from the leaf into the tree become trapped in the leaf with no fresh water to clean it. Not only does this cause the leaf to turn brown, eventually, but it also causes the cells within it to harden so much that the leaf tears and blows away. Thus the pile of leaves you enjoyed jumping in as a child.

Because each tree, and each leaf, contains a unique amount of nutrients depending on how well-nourished it was over the spring and summer, the way each leaf breaks down during the winter months is also quite different. The result is the unique and complex facet of colors we see in each neighborhood or forest each fall.

http://www.sciencemadesimple.com/leaves.htm

5. What is the main theme of the above passage?

Ⓐ Fall weather
Ⓑ What happens to the leaves during fall
Ⓒ The life cycle of a tree during fall
Ⓓ Weather during fall

6. What is the purpose of this excerpt? Circle the correct answer choice.

Ⓐ to explain why leaves change colors and drop from trees.
Ⓑ to describe the colors of leaves in the fall
Ⓒ to tell the reader about the North East part of the country
Ⓓ to define chlorophyl

History of Olympics
From Ancient Olympics Guide

Read the information below and answer the questions that follow.

Even though the modern Olympic Games are held every four years, they bear little resemblance to the athletic contests held at Olympia in Greece in ancient times. The games were open to competitors from all Greece, and the contests included chariot racing, horse racing, running, wrestling, boxing, and the pentathlon, a contest involving jumping, quoit throwing, javelin throwing, running and wrestling. Scholars date the earliest contests at 776 B.C., more than two and a half thousand years ago. The first trophies that were won consisted not of gold medals and cups but of simple crowns of olive leaves. Women and slaves were admitted neither as contestants nor as spectators. The classical games ceased to be held probably about A.D.393.

Much of the credit for the revival of the Games held at Athens in 1896 goes to Baron Pierre de Coubertin, a French classical scholar, who greatly admired the sporting ideals of the ancient Greeks. As an educationist and lover of amateurism, he looked upon physical exercise as an essential feature of a balanced education. Forty-two events were contested, and new disciplines such as cycling, hurdling, high jump, shooting, and gymnastics were introduced.

One of the most popular events of the modern Olympics is the marathon. This very tiring twenty six mile foot race over an open course is the supreme test of the runners' endurance. The marathon was not a part of the ancient Olympics although it originated in Greece.

And, finally, a more recent development in the Olympics is the introduction of the winter games, which were started in 1924. They are held separately from the summer games but in the same year. The Winter Olympics provide competition in skiing, speed and figure skating, ice hockey, and rifle shooting. Such cold weather sports could never have developed in the warm climate of Greece.

7. Choose a suitable alternate title for this passage.

Ⓐ The Winter Sports
Ⓑ The Games' Growth
Ⓒ How the Olympics Evolved
Ⓓ Popular Sports

Carnivorous Plant

Read the information below and answer the questions that follow.

Venus Fly Traps are difficult to locate because they are endangered. This means that even in the places where they grow the best, you'll find fewer and fewer plants. For a long time, people would go to these areas and dig up Venus Fly Traps to take home because they are so different and rare. Over time, the number of plants growing in the wild has gotten smaller. Now it's illegal to pick a Venus Fly Trap from the wild. In fact, if you do try and take one home, you could have to pay a fine of up to $2000! Because people still love to look at these unique plants, the Carolina Beach Park in North Carolina has created a safe preserve to grow, protect, and show off Venus Fly Traps.

8. What is the best summary of this paragraph? Circle the correct answer choice.

Ⓐ Venus Fly Traps are beautiful plants
Ⓑ Venus Fly Traps need special nutrients to grow and reproduce
Ⓒ Venus Fly Traps are endangered plants and there are laws to ensure their preservation
Ⓓ Venus Fly Traps are used to prepare delicious food items

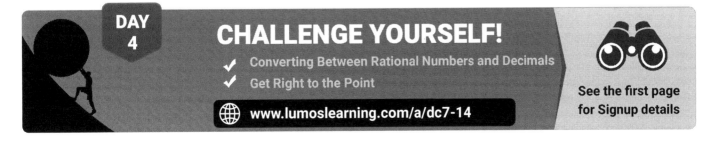

DAY 4

CHALLENGE YOURSELF!
✔ Converting Between Rational Numbers and Decimals
✔ Get Right to the Point

🌐 www.lumoslearning.com/a/dc7-14

See the first page for Signup details

1. Andrew has $9.39 but needs $15.00 to make a purchase. How much more does he need?

   Ⓐ $6.39
   Ⓑ $5.61
   Ⓒ $5.39
   Ⓓ $6.61

2. Ben has to unload a truck filled with 25 bags of grain for his horses. Each bag weighs 50.75 pounds.

   How many total pounds does he have to move?

   Ⓐ 12,687.50 pounds
   Ⓑ 1,268.75 pounds
   Ⓒ 126.875 pounds
   Ⓓ 1250 pounds

3. A Chinese restaurant purchased 1528.80 pounds of rice. If they received 50 identical bags, how much rice was in each bag?

   Ⓐ 30.576 pounds
   Ⓑ 305.76 pounds
   Ⓒ 3.0576 pounds
   Ⓓ None of the above.

4. Solve each equation and mark if the answer is negative, positive or zero.

	Negative	Zero	Positive
$-\dfrac{6}{7} - \left(-\dfrac{6}{7}\right)$	○	○	○
$-5 - \dfrac{3}{5}$	○	○	○
$\dfrac{3}{4} - \dfrac{1}{5}$	○	○	○

5. Which sentence below contains a conjunction indicating a possible relationship?

Ⓐ Due to the large number of offers, Mike had to increase his giveaway time limit.
Ⓑ Kelsey is coming to dinner and a movie with me tonight.
Ⓒ The oven did not cook right because the brownies were not completely done.
Ⓓ The promise of a better life brought many immigrants to America.

6. Which set of words lets the reader know a passage will include sequencing?

Ⓐ Finally, before, after that
Ⓑ Consequently, as a result, therefore
Ⓒ And, if, or
Ⓓ Neither, because of that, and

7. Which set of words lets the reader know a passage will include cause and effect?

Ⓐ Finally, before, after that
Ⓑ Consequently, as a result, therefore
Ⓒ And, if, or
Ⓓ Neither, because of that, and

The Assassination of President Lincoln
April 14, 1865

Read the information below and answer the questions that follow.

Shortly after 10 p.m. on April 14, 1865, actor, John Wilkes Booth entered the presidential box at Ford's Theatre in Washington D.C. and fatally shot President Abraham Lincoln. As Lincoln slumped forward in his seat, Booth leapt onto the stage and escaped through the back door. A doctor in the audience rushed over to examine the paralyzed president. Lincoln was then carried across the street to Petersen's Boarding House, where he died early the next morning.

Lincoln was the first president assassinated in U.S. history. Why did Booth do it? He thought it would aid the South, which had just surrendered to Federal forces. It had nearly the opposite effect, ending Lincoln's plans for a rather generous peace. Booth did not act alone. This "wanted" poster appeared everywhere, offering a reward for the arrest of Booth and his accomplices. The conspirators were all captured, and Booth was shot while trying to escape from Union soldiers.

The whole country grieved the death of President Lincoln. As the nine-car funeral train carried President Lincoln home for burial in Springfield, Illinois, people showed up at train stations all along the way to pay their respects.

"The Assassination of President Lincoln." The Assassination of President Lincoln. N.p., n.d. Web. 15 July 2013.

8. What happened last in the SECOND paragraph?

Use the below space for your drawing activity.

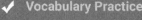

THIS WEEK'S ONLINE ACTIVITIES

✓ Reading Assignment   ✓ Vocabulary Practice

✓ Write Your Summer Diary

 www.lumoslearning.com/a/slh7-8

See the first page
for Signup details

WEEKLY FUN SUMMER PHOTO CONTEST

Take a picture of your summer fun activity and share it on Twitter or Instagram

Use the #SummerLearning mention

@LumosLearning on	@lumos.learning on
Twitter	**Instagram**

Tag friends and increase your chances of winning the contest.

PARTICIPATE AND STAND A CHANCE TO WIN $50 AMAZON GIFT CARD!

WEEK 4
SUMMER PRACTICE

1. **Ruby is two years younger than her brother. If Ruby's brother's age is A, which of the following expressions correctly represents Ruby's age?**

   Ⓐ A - 2
   Ⓑ A + 2
   Ⓒ 2A
   Ⓓ 2 - A

2. **Find the difference:** $8n - (3n-6) =$

   Ⓐ -n
   Ⓑ 5n - 6
   Ⓒ 5n + 6
   Ⓓ 8n - 6

3. **Find the sum:**

   $6t + (3t - 5) =$

   Ⓐ 9t - 5
   Ⓑ 9t + 5
   Ⓒ 3t - 5
   Ⓓ 6t - 5

4. **A bookstore is advertising $2 off the price of each book. You decide to buy 8 books. Let p represent the price of each book. Use the expression 8(p − 2) to find out how much you would spend if the regular price of each book is $13.**

   Write your answer in the box given below.

   [   ]

Read the information below and answer the questions that follow.

Scientists in South Korea have developed a type of artificial skin that will allow robots to feel slight vibrations. This skin, developed by weaving together extremely small nano hairs made of polymer or plastic, is more sensitive than human skin. When vibration is applied to this artificial skin, the nano hairs bend against each other to generate an electrical current. Sensors within the skin evaluate the current, and using that information determine the source of the vibration.

Researchers are excited about the potential for this new development. The artificial skin could be used to cover prosthetic limbs to help those who have lost a limb experience more realistic sensations and function more naturally.

http://en.wikipedia.org/wiki/Neuroplasticity

5. What can we assume about the nano hairs described in this article?

Ⓐ They are not made of natural or organic material.
Ⓑ They are made of the same material as human hair.
Ⓒ They generate electricity.
Ⓓ They were invented by South Korean scientists.

6. Based on this article, we can assume that prosthetic means...

Ⓐ Natural
Ⓑ Computerized
Ⓒ Artificial
Ⓓ Electrical

7. What is a sensor?

Ⓐ A device used to transmit a message
Ⓑ A means by which the body perceives an external stimulus; one of the faculties of sight, smell, hearing, taste, and touch.
Ⓒ A device that detects or measures a physical property and records, indicates, or otherwise responds to it.
Ⓓ An artificial limb used by those who have suffered an accident or disease.

Read the information below and answer the questions that follow.

Scientists in South Korea have developed a In the Class Novel section of your Reader's Notebook:

· Make a list of the most important characters in Someone Was Watching.

· Make a list of the most important characters in the AR book you're reading.

· Compare a character from each novel. Describe how the characters are alike. Be specific.

For example:

I'm reading a novel called Mockingjay. Katniss (the main character) is like Chris because they are both trying to protect someone they love. Katniss is trying to make the world a safer place and is not sure who she can trust. Chris is searching for the truth about his sister's disappearance, and is not sure who he can trust.

8. Part A
What does the document tell the reader to be specific about?

Ⓐ Comparing characters
Ⓑ Describing how the characters are alike and different
Ⓒ Comparing characters and describing how they are alike
Ⓓ Contrasting the characters traits

Part B
What is the reader supposed to do with the characters from Someone Was Watching?

Ⓐ make a list of books read
Ⓑ make a list of important characters
Ⓒ make a list characters in their own novel
Ⓓ make a list of items left to do

DAY 1

CHALLENGE YOURSELF!

✔ Applying Properties to Rational Expressions
✔ Getting Technical

🌐 www.lumoslearning.com/a/dc7-16

See the first page for Signup details

1. Which of the following expressions represents "5% of a number"?

   Ⓐ 5n
   Ⓑ 0.5n
   Ⓒ 0.05n
   Ⓓ 500n

2. Jill is shopping at a department store that is having a sale this week. The store has advertised 15% off certain off-season merchandise. Jill calculates the sales price by multiplying the regular price by 15% and then subtracting that amount from the regular price: SP = RP - 0.15(RP), where S = Sales Price and R = Regular Price. Find a simpler way for Jill to calculate the sales price as she shops.

   Ⓐ SP = 0.15 RP
   Ⓑ SP = 1.15RP
   Ⓒ SP = 0.85RP
   Ⓓ SP = 1.85RP

3. Rewrite the following expression for the perimeter of a rectangle.

   P = l + w + l + w, where P = perimeter, l = length, and w = width.

   Ⓐ P = l + 2w
   Ⓑ P = l + w
   Ⓒ P = 2(l) + w
   Ⓓ P = 2(l + w)

4. Which of the expressions have like terms? There are more than 1 correct answer. Select all the correct answer choices

   Ⓐ 4xy - 8y
   Ⓑ -7x + 3x
   Ⓒ h + 9.3h
   Ⓓ 5t + 5
   Ⓔ 12df - 3df
   Ⓕ 8x - 2y

Bushmen

Read the information below and answer the questions that follow.

Shortly after 10 p.m. on April 14, 1865, actor, With so much technology around us each day, it is hard to imagine that anyone in the world would live without television, let alone a cell phone or radio. Still, there are a few cultures that maintain an extremely primitive lifestyle, nearly untouched by the modern world. One of those is commonly known as the Bushmen of Kalahari.

The Bushmen, also known as the "Basarwa" or "San" is found throughout southern Africa in regions of the Kalahari Desert. Nomadic hunters and gatherers by nature, they roam the region living in small kinship groups and, relatively isolated from the rest of society, have developed an extremely unique culture not otherwise seen or understood by modern man.

Unlike English, which is built on a complex system of sounds and letters, the Bushmen speak an extremely unique language made exclusively of clicking sounds. The sounds are created with a sucking action from the tongue, and even the click language itself can vary widely from tribe to tribe, making it extremely difficult to communicate with non-Bush people.

In addition to language, the Bushmen have a very different way of living. Similar to Eskimos, groups of Bushmen will live in "kinship" societies. Led by their elders, they travel together, with women in the group gathering food while men hunt for it. Children, on the other hand, have no duties other than playing. In fact, leisure is an extremely important part of Bushmen society. Dance, music, and humor are essential, with a focus on family rather than technology or development. Because of this, some people associate the Bush culture with a backward kind of living or low status.

Because of the increased speed of advancement and urban development, the Bushmen culture is in danger. Some have already been forced to switch from hunting to farming due to modernization programs in their countries. Others have been forced to move to certain areas of their countries so that modernization can continue to occur there. With so much development, it's clear that though the Bushmen culture is very rich, it is also in danger of extinction. It is unclear how long the Bush culture will continue.

5. How are the paragraphs in this selection organized?

Ⓐ by topic
Ⓑ from broad ideas to narrow ideas
Ⓒ chronologically
Ⓓ compare and contrast

Read the information below and answer the questions that follow.

Looking for a new hobby? Do you like baseball? If you answered "yes" to these two questions, baseball card collecting might be a fun pastime for you to begin! Ever since candy and gum manufacturers started putting cards with pictures of popular baseball players into the packages in the 1800s to encourage young people to buy their sweets, kids have been collecting baseball cards. Now, more than 200 years later, baseball card collecting has become a popular hobby for children and adults alike.

What You Need to Be a Baseball Card Collector

The main thing you need to start a baseball card collection is cards, of course! Baseball cards are usually sold in packs of four or more cards. Large chain stores like Walmart and Target, as well as drug stores, are the easiest places to find packs of baseball cards. You can also find cards at special baseball card shops. You should plan on spending around $2.99 for each pack of baseball cards you purchase. Once you've started your collection by buying packs of cards, you'll probably find that there are one or two specific cards you want that you haven't been able to get in packs. The best places to get single cards are the baseball card shows held at malls or convention centers or on the Internet. You can also trade cards with another baseball card collector. A lot of times, a friend has the card you're looking for. Because you might also have a card he or she wants, trading is a great way to build the collection that you want. Plus, it doesn't cost you a cent!

As a baseball card collector, you'll not only need cards, but also a place to put them. Baseball cards can become very valuable. You may get a card in a pack today that is worth ten or twenty times the price you paid for it years down the line. The price that you can sell a baseball card is based on the condition that it is in. For this reason, you want to be sure to have a safe place to store your cards where they won't get damaged. There are lots of different options for storing baseball cards. If you have just a few important cards that you want to protect, you can purchase sleeves to store them in. Sleeves are firm plastic wrappers that are slightly larger than a card. You simply slip the card into the opening on the sleeve, and it is protected from wetness and bending. If you have several cards to store, consider buying boxes or albums. At baseball card shops, you can buy boxes that are specially designed to store baseball cards. For serious baseball card collectors with very valuable cards, cases that lock are the ideal spot to store your cards.

Once you've collected cards for a while, you'll want a way to keep track of what cards you have in your collection. Those with small collections can use a notebook where they write down the players' names and dates of the cards they have. For those with larger collections, the computer is the best place to keep track of their collections. While you can create your own database of cards using a software program on your computer, there are also special baseball card software programs that make it much easier. Beckett, the company that publishes a most popular guide to baseball card values, sells a computer program with the names of cards already loaded into it. You simply need to go in and click on the names of cards to record those that are part of your collection.

Types of Baseball Cards You Can Collect
There are four main companies that produce baseball cards: Topps, Upper Deck, Fleer, and Donruss/Playoff. The most popular and easi-

est cards to find in stores are those made by Topps and Upper Deck. Each of these companies sells sets of cards. You can either purchase a full set from a baseball card store or show, or you can put together a set by buying enough packs of cards to collect each card in the set. The basic set put out each year by each company is made up of 500 or more cards. Cards feature posed pictures of Major League Baseball players as well as action shots. Within the basic set, there are several subsets that each has a special theme. For example, a card set might have a special subset of homerun heroes within the larger basic set they sell that year. If you buy individual packs of baseball cards to build your set, you'll have a chance at getting insert cards. These are special cards that are printed in limited quantities and are inserted into packs. Insert cards are usually worth more money than basic cards because there are fewer of them produced each year.

For serious baseball collectors, there are premium and specialty cards available. Premium cards come in sets and are printed by the main baseball card companies. These cards are more expensive but feature extra perks. For example, parallel sets of premium cards are the same as the basic set but are fancier. They might have bolder colors or special borders. In addition to premium sets, serious baseball card collectors like to collect rookie cards. A rookie card is a player's first baseball card. The year that the player is placed on a team's roster, he becomes a rookie. Rookie cards become very valuable when the player goes on to have a successful career. Autographed baseball cards are another great find for devoted baseball card collectors. There are two types of autographed cards: those with autographs signed on the actual card and those with autographs cut from other sources that are glued onto the card. This second type is known as cut autos. Cut autos are usually created for players who are no longer living.

A new type of baseball card has just come out in the last few years and may totally change card collecting in the future. Digital baseball cards are now available. These cards don't come printed on paper like traditional baseball cards. Instead, they are purchased and stored on the Internet. One of the major companies, Topps, has already had great success with its line of computerbased cards called eTopps.

Whatever type of cards you choose to collect, you're sure to find hours of enjoyment in with your new hobby.

6. **If you wanted to find information about how to start a baseball card collection, which section of this selection would you want to read?**

    (A) what you need to be a baseball card collector
    (B) types of baseball cards you can collect
    (C) what companies make baseball cards
    (D) looking for a new hobby

Table of Contents for Flowers of the Farm

Read the information below and answer the questions that follow.

7. Based on this table of contents, what can you tell about how this book is organized?

Ⓐ The book is organized by types of flowers.
Ⓑ The book is organized by locations where the flowers can be found.
Ⓒ The book is organized chronologically.
Ⓓ The book is organized by location and type of flower found on the farm.

Cycling Tours of Brooklyn

Read the information below and answer the questions that follow.

Brooklyn is an exciting borough of New York City and offers much to see and do. Visitors can enjoy many different shops and restaurants, as well as parks, museums, and outside festivals. A great way to visit Brooklyn is by bicycle and "Get up and Ride," a cycling tour company, offers two different options.

The Classic Tour

Distance – 10 miles

Duration – 3 to 3.5 hours

Stops include – Greenpoint, Brooklyn Heights, and the Brooklyn Navy Yard

Food and Drink – Stop in the Dekalb Marketplace

Special features – Cyclists end the day with a ferry ride to Manhattan

Cost - $65

The Best of Brooklyn Tour

Distance – 15 miles

Duration - 5 hours

Stops – All of the stops on the classic tour, plus Clinton Hill and Fort Green

Food and Drink – Stop in Dekalb Marketplace

Special Features – Cyclists end with a ferry ride to Manhattan

Cost - $95

The tours can accommodate groups of up to eight people. Bicycles and safety equipment are provided. Tours run Tuesday through Saturday and leave from Brooklyn Heights.

8. **Based on the way it is formatted, this document is most likely a(n)_____ Circle the correct answer choice.**

   (A) Encyclopedia entry
   (B) Outline for an essay
   (C) Advertisement
   (D) Table of contents

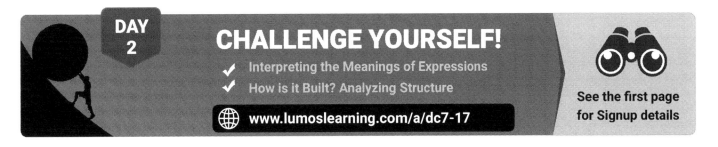

1. A 30 gallon overhead tank was slowly filled with water through a tap. The amount of water (W, in gallons) that is filled over a period of t hours can be found using W = 3.75(t). If the tap is opened at 7 AM and closed at 3 PM, how much water would be in the tank? Assume that the tank is empty before opening the tap.

   Ⓐ 18 gallons
   Ⓑ 20 gallons
   Ⓒ 24 gallons
   Ⓓ The tank is full

2. The ratio (by volume) of milk to water in a certain solution is 3 to 8. If the total volume of the solution is 187 cubic feet, what is the volume of water in the solution?

   Ⓐ 130 cubic feet
   Ⓑ 132 cubic feet
   Ⓒ 134 cubic feet
   Ⓓ 136 cubic feet

3. A box has a length of 12 inches and width of 10 inches. If the volume of the box is 960 cubic inches, what is its height?

   Ⓐ 6 inches
   Ⓑ 10 inches
   Ⓒ 12 inches
   Ⓓ 8 inches

4. Which equation correctly represents the model and what is the solution?

   Note: Select the answers that have the correct equation and solution. There is more than one correct answer.

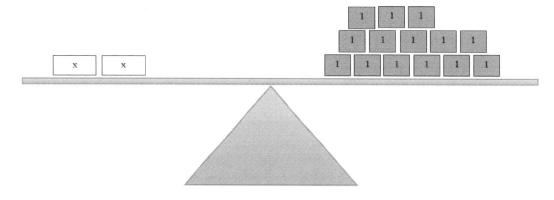

   Ⓐ 2x = 14 and x = 7
   Ⓑ x + 2 = 14 and x = 12
   Ⓒ 2 + x = 14 and x = 12
   Ⓓ x + x = 14 and x = 7
   Ⓔ 2 = 14x and x = 0.5

From Guiseppi Verdi by Thomas Trapper

Read the information below and answer the questions that follow.

Whenever the organ man came into the village of Roncole, in Italy (where Verdi was born, October 10, 1813), Verdi could not be kept indoors. But he followed the wonderful organ and the wonderful man who played it, all day long, as happy as he could be.

When Giuseppe was seven years old, his father, though only a poor innkeeper, bought him a spinet, a sort of small piano. So faithfully did the little boy practice that the spinet was soon quite worn out and new jacks, or hammers, had to be made for it. This was done by Stephen Cavaletti, who wrote a message on one of the jacks telling that he made them anew and covered them with leather, and fixed the pedal, doing all for nothing, because the little boy, Giuseppe Verdi, showed such willingness to practice and to learn. Thus the good Stephen thought this was pay enough.

5. Based on these paragraphs, what can you infer the author's view of Verdi is?

Ⓐ He is amazed by Verdi's talent.
Ⓑ He thinks Verdi started playing an instrument at too young of an age.
Ⓒ He is jealous of Verdi's talent.
Ⓓ He is unsure what to make of Verdi's talent.

The Great Round World and What's Going On In It magazine article

Read the information below and answer the questions that follow.

The Czar of Russia is quite ill, and everyone feels sorry that he should be sick now when his advice and assistance are so badly needed to settle the worrying Turkish question, which has so troubled Europe.

The young Czar Nicholas, who was crowned with so much pomp and glory at Moscow last August, seems unable to carry on the government of Russia.

Many people say he is too weak to govern, and that there are going to be troubles and revolts in Russia.

The truth of the matter seems to be, that the young Czar is a gentle, kind-hearted man, who will not govern Russia in the stern, cruel way that his forefathers have done, and who is therefore thought to be weak and incapable.

While he is making a part of his people love him for his goodness, by far the larger half, who have, under the old rule, been able to make money and gain great power, are furious against him.

Poor young Nicholas is not only hated by the people who were most friendly to his father, but by the Nihilists, who look upon him as their natural enemy, and, between the two parties, it is said that the Czar goes about in constant fear of his life.

Nicholas never wanted to be a ruler. Those who know him say that he has become grave and sad in the few months since he came to the throne.

It is said that he is of too gentle a disposition to be able to keep his ministers in order and that they quarrel fiercely in his presence, and show very little respect for him.

According to all accounts, his health is giving way under the constant worry, and it is reported that he received a shock a few weeks ago, which so completely upset him, that it brought on his present illness.

He was walking in his gardens, and wishing to speak to one of the men who was at work; he signaled to him to come to him. The gardener, proud of his sovereign's notice, ran towards him at full speed. But a sentry, who had not noticed the Czar's signal, fearing that the man was going to harm the Emperor, fired his gun at him, and he fell dead at the Czar's feet.

Nicholas was terribly overcome by the dreadful mistake.

Some people say that his present illness is due to anxiety about the Czarina, who is also ill, and again others say that the wound which Nicholas received when he was traveling in Japan is the cause.

He was struck by a crazy Japanese, and would have been killed, had not Prince George of Greece, the son of the present King of Greece, who was with him, warded off the blow. As it was, the blow was heavy enough to form a lump on the young man's skull, which has caused him great pain, and which some people declare is troubling him now.

Whatever the cause, the Czar is ill, and in no state to attend to anything but his own affairs. It is a sad pity just at this moment when Europe needs him so badly.

6. What is the author's view of Czar Nicholas?

Ⓐ The author does not have much respect for Nicholas.
Ⓑ The author feels sympathy and pity for Nicholas.
Ⓒ The author thinks that Nicholas has no business being a Czar.
Ⓓ The author thinks Russia is worse off now that Czar Nicholas is its ruler.

Advertisement from The Great Round World and What's Going On In It magazine -- Anonymous author

Read the information below and answer the questions that follow.

School and College Text-Books
AT WHOLESALE PRICES
At my New Store (FEBRUARY 1ST)
3 & 5 West 18th Street, The St. Ann Building
With the greatly increased facilities, I can now offer to my customers the convenience of an assortment of text books and supplies more complete than any other in any store in this city. Books will be classified according to subject. Teachers and students are invited to call and refer to the shelves when in search of information; every convenience and assistance will be rendered them.

Reading Charts, miscellaneous Reference Charts, Maps, Globes, Blackboards, and School Supplies at net prices singly or in quantity.

All books removed from old store (more or less damaged by removal) will be closed out at low prices.

Mail orders promptly attended to
All books, etc., subject to approval
William Beverley Harrison, 3 & 5 West 18th Street
FORMERLY 59 FIFTH AVENUE

7. What is the author's point of view in this ad?

Ⓐ His new store is even better than his old store.
Ⓑ His store has some of the books teachers and students need.
Ⓒ His books are now available by mail order.
Ⓓ His store has moved to a new location.

Diabetic Help

Read the information below and answer the questions that follow.

Researchers at pharmaceutical company Eli Lilly and an association that places assistance dogs in Indianapolis, IN, are working together on an exciting new project that will study how dogs are able to detect low blood sugar in their diabetic owners. Diabetics suffer from a condition by which the pancreas does not produce enough insulin to maintain a healthy level of blood glucose. If a diabetic person's blood glucose level drops too low, he or she may become unconscious or even go into a coma.

One dog who has had a lot of success in identifying low blood sugar is a two-year-old named Pete. Pete, like all dogs, has a sense of smell 10,000 times more sensitive than that of humans. Pete's owner is a scientist with Eli Lilly, and she is trying to figure out what is inside a dog's nose that makes it possible to smell low blood sugar. If the researcher can figure out how to reproduce that kind of sensitivity, more diabetic people can be protected from the consequences of low blood sugar.

Until the researchers isolate what is inside Pete's nose, the Indiana Canine Assistance Network will continue to train dogs like Pete. It's a slow and expensive process, though. In the last ten years, the organization has trained 100 dogs, and the training has cost $25,000 or more for each dog.

8. In which of the following types of writing are author's beliefs NOT important? Circle the correct answer choice.

Ⓐ Political speech
Ⓑ Advertisement
Ⓒ News report
Ⓓ Job resume

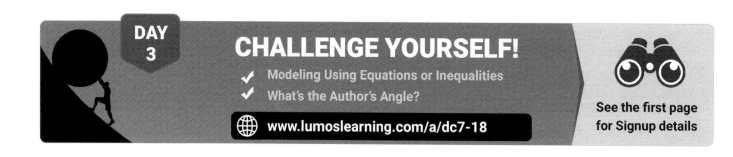

DAY 3

CHALLENGE YOURSELF!
✔ Modeling Using Equations or Inequalities
✔ What's the Author's Angle?

🌐 www.lumoslearning.com/a/dc7-18

See the first page for Signup details

1. Bob, the plumber, charges 1/4 the cost of materials as his labor fee. If his current job has a material cost of $130, how much will Bob charge his client (including his labor fee)?

Ⓐ $162.50
Ⓑ $32.50
Ⓒ $130.25
Ⓓ None of the above

2. A box has a length of 6x inches. The width equals one third the length, and the height equals half the length. If the volume equals 972 cubic inches, what does x equal?

Ⓐ 5
Ⓑ 2
Ⓒ 3
Ⓓ 4

3. Taylor is trimming the shrubbery along three sides of his backyard. The backyard is rectangular in shape. The length of the backyard is twice its width and the total perimeter is 180 feet.

The shrubbery that Taylor needs to trim is along three sides of the rectangular backyard (along the two lengths and one width). Find the total length of the shrubbery that he needs to trim.

Ⓐ 180 ft
Ⓑ 60 ft
Ⓒ 90 ft
Ⓓ 150 ft

4. Which expression is the product of two factors and is equivalent to 3x - 27. Circle the correct answer choice.

Ⓐ 3 (x - 9)
Ⓑ -3 (3x -9)
Ⓒ 8x (8x - 15)
Ⓓ 3x (9x8)

Fall Leaves
USDA Forest Service

Read the information below and answer the questions that follow.

We almost always think of trees as being green, but there is one time of year when their leaves turn a myriad orange, red, yellow, and brown: the beautiful and chilly days of fall. Those living in the Eastern or Northern United States come to anticipate the change in color starting in September or October every single year. But what causes the leaves to change color, and why?

Just like many animals that hibernate for the winter, trees experience a unique change during the winter months. During summer, for instance, plants use the process of photosynthesis to transform carbon dioxide found in the air into organic compounds like sugars using energy from the sun. During the winter, however, there is less light to go around, and their ability to create food from the photosynthesis process is limited.

What does that have to do with a leaf's color? The substance that allows trees to turn carbon dioxide into food (chlorophyll) is also the cause of the leaf's green sheen. As the photosynthesis process wanes in the colder months due to the lack of sun, so does its greenish hue, allowing other elements present in the leaf to show through. Believe it or not, the yellows and oranges that appear in fall have actually been there all year in the form of nutrients like carotene (also found in carrots). The intense green color of the chlorophyll had simply overshadowed them. But what about the reds and browns? And what causes the leaves to fall away after they change color?

The bright reds and purples in each leaf come from a strong antioxidant that many trees create on their own because of their protective qualities. The antioxidant helps protect the trees from the sun, lower their freezing levels, and protect them from frost. As winter comes, so does the need for the antioxidant (similar to the way a dog gets more fur during winter to stay warmer).

As for the leaves falling, that is another story. At the base of each leaf, there is a layer of cells that carry food and water from the leaf to the tree during the summer months to keep it fed. In the fall, that layer actually starts to harden, preventing the passage of nutrients. Because of this, the nutrients and waste that previously passed from the leaf into the tree become trapped in the leaf with no fresh water to clean it. Not only does this cause the leaf to turn brown, eventually, but it also causes the cells within it to harden so much that the leaf tears and blows away. Thus the pile of leaves you enjoyed jumping in as a child.

Because each tree, and each leaf, contains a unique amount of nutrients depending on how well-nourished it was over the spring and summer, the way each leaf breaks down during the winter months is also quite different. The result is the unique and complex facet of colors we see in each neighborhood or forest each fall.

5. If this passage was turned into a video documentary, what would it include to help you understand how the leaves change color?

Ⓐ Time-lapse video of the leaves changing color
Ⓑ Paintings by artists depicting fall leaves
Ⓒ Pictures of animals that hibernate during the winter
Ⓓ Subtitles of the text on the screen

6. You've been asked to turn this passage into a slide show presentation. Which graphic would you use to help explain the process of leaves changing color?

Ⓐ A picture of leaves that have changed color
Ⓑ A picture of animals hibernating
Ⓒ A diagram of the process leaves go through when changing color
Ⓓ A diagram explaining when leaves change color around the world

7. A naturalist is presenting this information to a class of students. Which visual aid could she bring to help students understand the information in the passage?

Ⓐ A picture of leaves that have changed color
Ⓑ A pile of leaves of different colors
Ⓒ A photograph of a pile of leaves
Ⓓ A diagram explaining the process

From Guiseppi Verdiby Thomas Trapper

Read the information below and answer the questions that follow.

Whenever the organ man came into the village of Roncole, in Italy (where Verdi was born, October 10, 1813), Verdi could not be kept indoors. But he followed the wonderful organ and the wonderful man who played it, all day long, as happy as he could be.

When Giuseppe was seven years old, his father, though only a poor innkeeper, bought him a spinet, a sort of small piano. So faithfully did the little boy practice that the spinet was soon quite worn out and new jacks, or hammers, had to be made for it. This was done by Stephen Cavaletti, who wrote a message on one of the jacks telling that he made them anew and covered them with leather, and fixed the pedal, doing all for nothing, because the little boy, Giuseppe Verdi, showed such willingness to practice and to learn. Thus the good Stephen thought this was pay enough.

8. If turned into a media production, this passage would most likely be...?

Ⓐ A story on the local news
Ⓑ A play at the local theater
Ⓒ A slideshow presentation
Ⓓ A song about Verdi

DAY 4

CHALLENGE YOURSELF!
✔ Solving Multi-Step Problems
✔ Comparing with Media

🌐 www.lumoslearning.com/a/dc7-19

See the first page
for Signup details

1. The annual salary for a certain position depends upon the years of experience of the applicant. The base salary is $50,000, and an additional $3,000 is added to that per year of experience, y, in the field. The company does not want to pay more than $70,000 for this position, though. Which of the following inequalities correctly expresses this scenario?

   Ⓐ $53,000y \leq 70,000$
   Ⓑ $3,000y \leq 50,000$
   Ⓒ $50,000 + 3,000y \leq 70,000$
   Ⓓ $3,000 + 50,000y \leq 70,000$

2. Huck has $225 in savings, and he is able to save an additional $45 per week from his work income. He wants to save enough money to have at least $500 in his savings. If w is the number of weeks, express this situation as an inequality.

   Ⓐ $265w \geq 500$
   Ⓑ $225 + 45w \geq 500$
   Ⓒ $225 \leq 45w$
   Ⓓ $225 + 45w \leq 500$

3. Lucy is charging her phone. It has a 20% charge right now and increases by an additional 2% charge every 3 minutes. She doesn't want to take it off the charger until it is at least 75% charged. If m is the number of minutes Lucy keeps her phone for charging, express this situation in an inequality.

   Ⓐ $20 + \dfrac{2}{3} m \leq 75$

   Ⓑ $20m + \dfrac{2}{3} m \leq 75$

   Ⓒ $75 + \dfrac{2}{3} m \geq 20$

   Ⓓ $20 + \dfrac{2}{3} m \geq 75$

4. A garden center sells 21 trays of red flowers, 12 trays of yellow flowers, and 16 trays of pink flowers every day. The gardener wants to know how many days, d, it will take to sell more than 200 trays of flowers. Which inequality models the situation.

   Circle the correct answer choice.

   Ⓐ $21d + 12d + 16d < 200$
   Ⓑ $21d + 12d + 16d > 200$
   Ⓒ $200 \leq 21d + 16d + 12d$
   Ⓓ $200 \geq 21d + 16d + 12d$

Fall Leaves
USDA Forest Service

Read the information below and answer the questions that follow.

We almost always think of trees as being green, but there is one time of year when their leaves turn a myriad orange, red, yellow, and brown: the beautiful and chilly days of fall. Those living in the Eastern or Northern United States come to anticipate the change in color starting in September or October every single year. But what causes the leaves to change color, and why?

Just like many animals that hibernate for the winter, trees experience a unique change during the winter months. During summer, for instance, plants use the process of photosynthesis to transform carbon dioxide found in the air into organic compounds like sugars using energy from the sun. During the winter, however, there is less light to go around, and their ability to create food from the photosynthesis process is limited.

What does that have to do with a leaf's color? The substance that allows trees to turn carbon dioxide into food (chlorophyll) is also the cause of the leaf's green sheen. As the photosynthesis process wanes in the colder months due to the lack of sun, so does its greenish hue, allowing other elements present in the leaf to show through. Believe it or not, the yellows and oranges that appear in fall have actually been there all year in the form of nutrients like carotene (also found in carrots). The intense green color of the chlorophyll had simply overshadowed them. But what about the reds and browns? And what causes the leaves to fall away after they change color?

The bright reds and purples in each leaf come from a strong antioxidant that many trees create on their own because of their protective qualities. The antioxidant helps protect the trees from the sun, lower their freezing levels, and protect them from frost. As winter comes, so does the need for the antioxidant (similar to the way a dog gets more fur during winter to stay warmer).

As for the leaves falling, that is another story. At the base of each leaf, there is a layer of cells that carry food and water from the leaf to the tree during the summer months to keep it fed. In the fall, that layer actually starts to harden, preventing the passage of nutrients. Because of this, the nutrients and waste that previously passed from the leaf into the tree become trapped in the leaf with no fresh water to clean it. Not only does this cause the leaf to turn brown, eventually, but it also causes the cells within it to harden so much that the leaf tears and blows away. Thus the pile of leaves you enjoyed jumping in as a child.

Because each tree, and each leaf, contains a unique amount of nutrients depending on how well-nourished it was over the spring and summer, the way each leaf breaks down during the winter months is also quite different. The result is the unique and complex facet of colors we see in each neighborhood or forest each fall.

5. **For the information in this selection to be considered reliable, it would need to be written by....**

Ⓐ a journalist
Ⓑ a student
Ⓒ a scientist
Ⓓ an environmental activist

Egyptian Pyramids

Read the information below and answer the questions that follow.

We almost always think of trees as being To-day, we have high-tech cranes and other machines to help us create massive skyscrapers and other modern works of architecture. Still, some of the most breathtaking architecture in the world, such as the ancient pyramids of Egypt, were created before those high-tech machines even existed. So how did those ancient civilizations create them?

Believe it or not, though they are one of the most studied and admired relics in history, there is no evidence to tell historians exactly how the Ancient Egyptians built the pyramids. Thus, they have been left to create their own theories as to how Egyptians created such amazing and awe-inspiring works of art.

According to one theory, the Egyptians placed logs under the large stone blocks in order to roll or transport them to the pyramid building location. Large groups of men would work to push or pull them into place (although historians also disagree on whether these men were slaves or skilled artisans). Still more, once the men moved the blocks to the pyramid location, they needed to lift them to ever-increasing heights to reach the top levels of the pyramid as it grew. Without modern cranes, many scientists have been baffled as to how they were able to do it. Some believe they used a ramp system that would allow them to roll the blocks upward around or through the pyramids; others believe they must have used a combination of pulleys and lifts. Still, most agree that once they did, they used a mixture of gravel and limestone to help fill any crevices and hold the mound together. With such a primitive yet impressive building process, it's obvious that the pyramids must have taken a great deal of time to build. With an estimated 2 million blocks weighing an average of 2.5 million tons each, the Great Pyramid of Giza, for instance, is estimated to have taken some 20 years to build. At 481 feet tall, it held the record of tallest building for 3,800 years – not bad for a building created almost entirely by hand.

Even though scientists don't know exactly how the Egyptians did it, they do know that the method the Egyptians used to build pyramids changed over time. In the early days, the pyramids were made completely of stone, with limestone used to create the main body and higher quality limestone being used for the smooth outer casing. Later on, the pyramids were made mostly of mud brick with a limestone casing. Though they were likely much easier to build, they didn't stand up nearly as well over time, leaving archaeologists with even fewer clues about their creation.

6. How could you verify whether or not the information in this selection is accurate?

Ⓐ by interviewing the author of the essay
Ⓑ by reading an encyclopedia entry on the Egyptian pyramids
Ⓒ by talking with an Egyptian historian
Ⓓ by going to Egypt

from The Great Round World and What's Going On In It magazine

Read the information below and answer the questions that follow.

The Czar of Russia is quite ill, and everyone feels sorry that he should be sick now when his advice and assistance are so badly needed to settle the worrying Turkish question, which has so troubled Europe.

The young Czar Nicholas, who was crowned with so much pomp and glory at Moscow last August, seems unable to carry on the government of Russia.
Many people say he is too weak to govern, and that there are going to be troubles and revolts in Russia.

The truth of the matter seems to be, that the young Czar is a gentle, kind-hearted man, who will not govern Russia in the stern, cruel way that his forefathers have done, and who is therefore thought to be weak and incapable.

While he is making a part of his people love him for his goodness, by far the larger half, who have, under the old rule, been able to make money and gain great power, are furious against him.

Poor young Nicholas is not only hated by the people who were most friendly to his father, but by the Nihilists, who look upon him as their natural enemy, and, between the two parties, it is said that the Czar goes about in constant fear of his life.

Nicholas never wanted to be a ruler. Those who know him say that he has become grave and sad in the few months since he came to the throne.
It is said that he is of too gentle a disposition to be able to keep his ministers in order and that they quarrel fiercely in his presence, and show very little respect for him.

According to all accounts, his health is giving way under the constant worry, and it is reported that he received a shock a few weeks ago, which so completely upset him, that it brought on his present illness.

He was walking in his gardens, and wishing to speak to one of the men who was at work; he signaled to him to come to him. The gardener, proud of his sovereign's notice, ran towards him at full speed. But a sentry, who had not noticed the Czar's signal, fearing that the man was going to harm the Emperor, fired his gun at him, and he fell dead at the Czar's feet.

Nicholas was terribly overcome by the dreadful mistake.

Some people say that his present illness is due to anxiety about the Czarina, who is also ill, and again others say that the wound which Nicholas received when he was traveling in Japan is the cause.

He was struck by a crazy Japanese, and would have been killed, had not Prince George of Greece, the son of the present King of Greece, who was with him, warded off the blow. As it was, the blow was heavy enough to form a lump on the young man's skull, which has caused him great pain, andwhich some people declare is troubling him now.

Whatever the cause, the Czar is ill, and in no state to attend to anything but his own affairs. It is a sad pity just at this moment when Europe needs him so badly.

7. Which statement from this selection is a fact?

Ⓐ Many people say he is too weak to govern, and that there are going to be troubles and revolts in Russia.

Ⓑ The truth of the matter seems to be, that the young Czar is a gentle, kind-hearted man, who will not govern Russia in the stern, cruel way that his forefathers have done, and who is therefore thought to be weak and incapable.

Ⓒ According to all accounts, his health is giving way.

Ⓓ Nicholas was terribly overcome by the dreadful mistake.

Cycling Tours of Brooklyn

Read the information below and answer the questions that follow.

Brooklyn is an exciting borough of New York City and offers much to see and do. Visitors can enjoy many different shops and restaurants, as well as parks, museums, and outside festivals. A great way to visit Brooklyn is by bicycle and "Get up and Ride," a cycling tour company, offers two different options.

The Classic Tour

Distance – 10 miles

Duration – 3 to 3.5 hours

Stops include – Greenpoint, Brooklyn Heights, and the Brooklyn Navy Yard

Food and Drink – Stop in the Dekalb Marketplace

Special features – Cyclists end the day with a ferry ride to Manhattan

Cost - $65

The Best of Brooklyn Tour

Distance – 15 miles

Duration - 5 hours

Stops – All of the stops on the classic tour, plus Clinton Hill and Fort Green

Food and Drink – Stop in Dekalb Marketplace

Special Features – Cyclists end with a ferry ride to Manhattan

Cost - $95

The tours can accommodate groups of up to eight people. Bicycles and safety equipment are provided. Tours run Tuesday through Saturday and leave from Brooklyn Heights.

8. **What does the writer of this advertisement assume about the readers? Circle the correct answer choice.**

Ⓐ They have visited Brooklyn before.
Ⓑ They live in Manhattan.
Ⓒ They own bicycles.
Ⓓ They know how to ride a bicycle.

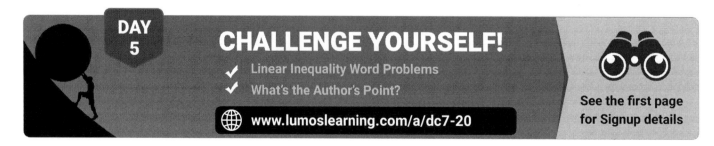

DAY 5

CHALLENGE YOURSELF!
✓ Linear Inequality Word Problems
✓ What's the Author's Point?

🌐 www.lumoslearning.com/a/dc7-20

See the first page for Signup details

DOWNHILL SKIING: SEVEN CRUCIAL WAYS TO IMPROVE YOUR SKILLS ON THE SLOPES

Downhill Skiing is a sport that requires keen balance, powerful leg strength, and a bit of courage -- to say the least.

When first starting out, it can be a bit daunting for beginners to know where to start, not to mention the fear of falling and getting hurt. This guide will help any novice Downhill skier to improve their skills and become more confident with their abilities on the mountain.

1. Improve Your Balance

As you might imagine, balance is a fundamental skill to have for any skier: if you can't balance well, you won't go far in the sport.

While you might be able to balance on one leg when standing, it is a completely different story when you are sliding down a hill with long planks attached to your boots.

Although it might not be the funniest thing to do, drills on flat ground or the "bunny hill" will help you improve your balance.

To start, you can try the "balance on one side drill," whereby you stand on one ski, lift your other foot off the ground, and propel yourself forward with your poles -- using what is called the double pull (pushing down on both poles simultaneously).

Do this for thirty seconds or so, then switch legs. You'll find that over time, your stability will gradually improve.

2. Build Strength in your Upper Legs

The constant maneuvering necessary when skiing will make even the strongest legs feel like noodles. To last longer on the hills and become more powerful on the powder, you should strengthen your legs by doing squats.

Start standing with your feet shoulder-width apart. Let your body drop slowly while keeping your weight on your heels, your hips back, and your back straight and at a slight forward angle.
Do the reverse and push yourself back up, maintaining the same form, and repeat as many times as you can. Although your legs will burn, push past the pain for the best results.

3. Increase your Calf Endurance

Calve-ups is a great way to make your calves more muscular. Simply find some stairs or a ledge and stand with the heel hanging off the edge.

THIS WEEK'S ONLINE ACTIVITIES

✔ Reading Assignment   ✔ Vocabulary Practice
✔ Write Your Summer Diary

🌐 www.lumoslearning.com/a/slh7-8

See the first page for Signup details

WEEKLY FUN SUMMER PHOTO CONTEST

📷 Take a picture of your summer fun activity and share it on Twitter or Instagram

Use the #SummerLearning mention

\#

@LumosLearning on	@lumos.learning on
🐦	📷
Twitter	**Instagram**

👥 Tag friends and increase your chances of winning the contest.

PARTICIPATE AND STAND A CHANCE TO WIN $50 AMAZON GIFT CARD!

WEEK 5
SUMMER PRACTICE

1. Triangle ABC and triangle PQR are similar. Find the value of x.

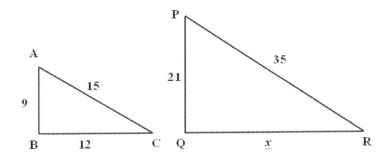

- Ⓐ 23
- Ⓑ 25
- Ⓒ 26
- Ⓓ 28

2. If the sides of two similar figures have a similarity ratio of $\dfrac{3}{2}$ what is the ratio of their areas?

Ⓐ $\dfrac{9}{4}$

Ⓑ $\dfrac{3}{2}$

Ⓒ $\dfrac{1}{3}$

Ⓓ $\dfrac{3}{1}$

3. **What is the similarity ratio between the following two similar figures?**

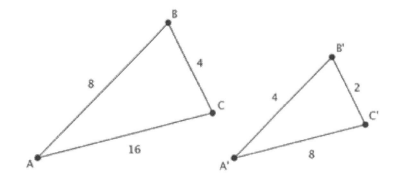

Ⓐ $\dfrac{2}{1}$

Ⓑ $\dfrac{1}{4}$

Ⓒ $\dfrac{2}{3}$

Ⓓ $\dfrac{3}{3}$

4 **On a map, 1 inch equals 15 miles. Two cities are 6 inches apart on the map. What is the actual distance between the cities? Write your answer in the box given below**

Read the information below and answer the questions that follow.

PASSAGE A:

When I was in the fourth grade, no one liked me because my brother was arrested, and that made everyone think that I might do something illegal too. It hurt my feelings to have to sit through school every day and not talk to anyone. When it was time to work in groups, I would have to sit with a group of kids that I knew hated me. Sometimes they would say something mean or move a chair away when it looked like I might sit with them. It was worse during lunch and on the bus when kids would yell things about my brother and ask me if I visited him in prison. After a while, I didn't want to go to school anymore, and I pretended to be sick every day, so I could stay home. Telling my parents and my teachers didn't change anything. After a while, my parents decided to let me change schools. The first year at my new school was bad because I didn't know anyone and was afraid to talk to people because of everything that happened at the old school. After a while, I made a few friends, and I started to feel better about talking to people. Now I have a few friends, and I don't feel like people are bullying me anymore.

PASSAGE B:

According to Dr. Norman Anderson, CEO of the American Psychological Association, bullying is any kind of aggressive behavior in which someone intentionally tries to harm or cause discomfort to another person. Bullying can be in the form of physical contact but is just as frequently demonstrated in cruel remarks, intentional exclusion of the victim, or in recent years, cyberbullying, in which the aggressor lashes out to the victim via e-mail, social networking, or text messaging.

There is no single, identifiable cause of bullying. Bullying often occurs as a result of influences from peer groups, family groups, communities, or even the media. It is, therefore, important to engage all of these groups if any anti-bullying effort is to be successful.

For many years, the primary means employed by schools to deal with the student to student bullying has been to punish the aggressor. Research has shown that disciplinary consequences alone will not significantly curb bullying in academic settings. Faculty and administrators must be trained to identify early warning signs that students are either bullies or being bullied, and onlookers, students who are not bullies themselves, but do nothing to inhibit bullying they witness, must be empowered with interpersonal skills training to help them intervene when they witness bullying within their peer groups.

5. **According the author of Passage B, what strategy would most likely have helped the author of Passage A?**

   Ⓐ Disciplinary consequences for the bullies
   Ⓑ Changing schools
   Ⓒ Training "onlookers" to intervene when they witness bullying
   Ⓓ Counseling for the bullying victim

6. What information from Passage B best explains this line from Passage A:

Telling my parents and my teachers didn't change anything.

- Ⓐ Faculty and administrators must be trained to identify early warning signs that students are either bullies or being bullied.
- Ⓑ Bullying often occurs as a result of influences from peer groups, family groups, community, or even the media.
- Ⓒ Bullying can be in the form of physical contact, but is just as frequently demonstrated in cruel remarks, intentional exclusion of the victim, or in recent years, cyber bullying, in which the aggressor lashes out to the victim via e-mail, social networking, or text messaging.
- Ⓓ For many years, the primary means employed by schools to deal with student to student bullying has been to punish the aggressor.

7. Which passage was most likely written by a middle school student?

- Ⓐ Passage A
- Ⓑ Passage B
- Ⓒ Both passages
- Ⓓ There is not enough information to determine the authors.

Read the information below and answer the questions that follow.

One should guard against preaching to young people success in the customary form as the main aim in life. The most important motive for work in school and in life is pleasure in work, pleasure in a result, and the knowledge of the value of the result to the community.

- Albert Einstein

The way to learn to do things is to do things. The way to learn a trade is to work at it. Success teaches how to succeed. Begin with the determination to succeed, and the work is half-done already.

- Henry Ford

"What Constitutes Success"
By Bessie Stanley (1905)

He has achieved success who has lived well,
laughed often and loved much;
who has gained the respect of intelligent men
and the love of little children;
who has filled his niche and accomplished his task;
who has left the world better than he found it,
whether by an improved poppy, a perfect poem, or a rescued soul;

who has never lacked appreciation of earth's beauty
or failed to express it;
who has always looked for the best in others
and given them the best he had;
whose life was an inspiration;
whose memory a benediction.

Steve Jobs, the CEO of Apple Computer, once said, "Being the richest man in the cemetery doesn't matter to me...Going to bed at night saying I've done something wonderful...that's what matters to me."

8. Which of the expressions about success above most closely align with Jobs' idea?

Ⓐ Albert Einstein
Ⓑ Henry Ford
Ⓒ Bessie Stanley
Ⓓ Both B and C.

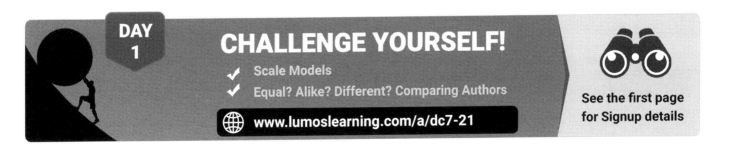

DAY
1

CHALLENGE YOURSELF!

✔ Scale Models
✔ Equal? Alike? Different? Comparing Authors

🌐 www.lumoslearning.com/a/dc7-21

See the first page
for Signup details

1. **Which of the following lengths cannot be the lengths of the sides of a triangle?**

   Ⓐ 4, 6, 9
   Ⓑ 3, 4, 2
   Ⓒ 2, 2, 3
   Ⓓ 1, 1, 2

2. **Which of the following set of lengths cannot be the lengths of the sides of a triangle?**

   Ⓐ 12.5, 20, 30
   Ⓑ 10, 10, 12
   Ⓒ 4, 8.5, 14
   Ⓓ 3, 3, 3

3. **If the measure of two angles in a triangle are 60 and 100 degrees, what is the measure of the third angle?**

   Ⓐ 20 degrees
   Ⓑ 50 degrees
   Ⓒ 30 degrees
   Ⓓ 180 degrees

4. **Which of these geometric shapes have exactly one pair of parallel sides?**

   Please write the correct answer from the list below into the box provided.

   Rhombus

   Triangle

   Regular Octagon

   Trapezoid

5. What type of word group is the following?

Walking down the street

(A) Phrase
(B) Dependent Clause
(C) Independent Clause
(D) Dependent Phrase

6. What type of word group is the underlined portion of the following sentence?

After leaving school, <u>I realized I left my science textbook in my locker.</u>

(A) Phrase
(B) Dependent Clause
(C) Independent Clause
(D) Complete Phrase

7. What type of word group is the underlined portion of the following sentence?

<u>Next Saturday</u>, my family is going to the beach.

(A) Phrase
(B) Dependent Clause
(C) Independent Clause
(D) Complete Clause

8. What type of word group is the underlined portion of the following sentence?

<u>Carley and Lori both bought their prom dresses from the same boutique</u> and their shoes from the same shoe store.

DAY
2

CHALLENGE YOURSELF!
✔ Drawing Plane (2-D) Figures
✔ Phrases and Clauses are Coming to Town

🌐 www.lumoslearning.com/a/dc7-22

See the first page
for Signup details

1. The horizontal cross section of a square pyramid is a _____.

    Ⓐ Square
    Ⓑ Circle
    Ⓒ Trapezoid
    Ⓓ Triangle

2. In order for a three-dimensional shape to be classified as a "prism," its horizontal cross-sections must be _____.

    Ⓐ congruent polygons
    Ⓑ non-congruent polygons
    Ⓒ circles
    Ⓓ equilateral triangles

3. Which of the following nets is NOT the net of a cube?

    Ⓐ

    Ⓑ

    Ⓒ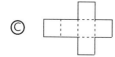

    Ⓓ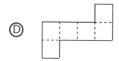

4. Match the cross section with the description of the shape of the cross section.

	Rectangle	Square
Horizontal cross section of a rectangular prism	○	○
Vertical cross section of a rectangular prism	○	○
Horizontal cross section of a square pyramid	○	○
Vertical cross section of a cube	○	○

5. Which of the following verb forms correctly fills in the blank in the following sentence?

Almost everybody _____ glad we do not have school next Monday.

Ⓐ is
Ⓑ are
Ⓒ were
Ⓓ am

6. Which of the following sentences has correct subject-verb agreement?

Ⓐ Each of my sisters have their rooms.
Ⓑ Marco's car needs a new transmission and a new clutch.
Ⓒ My cat don't fit through the kitty door because its stomach is so fat.
Ⓓ Drinking water help you lose weight.

7. Which of the following verb forms correctly fills in the blank in the following sentence?

Even though Randy _____ tomatoes, he loves spaghetti sauce.

Ⓐ hate
Ⓑ hates
Ⓒ hated
Ⓓ like

8. Which version of this sentence has correct subject-verb agreement? Circle the correct answer choice.

Ⓐ At the end of the rainbow was a leprechaun and a pot of gold.
Ⓑ At the end of the rainbow were a leprechaun and a pot of gold.
Ⓒ At the end of the rainbow is a leprechaun and a pot of gold.

DAY 3

CHALLENGE YOURSELF!
✔ Cross Sections of 3-D Figures
✔ Good Sentences are Built on Agreement

🌐 www.lumoslearning.com/a/dc7-23

See the first page
for Signup details

1. A circle is divided into 4 equal sections. What is the measure of each of the angles formed at the center of the circle?

   Ⓐ 25 degree
   Ⓑ 180 degree
   Ⓒ 90 degree
   Ⓓ 360 degree

2. What is the area of a circle with diameter 8 cm? Round your answer to the nearest tenth. Use π = 3.14.

   Ⓐ 201.1 cm²
   Ⓑ 201.0 cm²
   Ⓒ 50.2 cm²
   Ⓓ 25.1 cm²

3. What is the radius of a circle with a circumference of 125 cm? Round your answer to the nearest whole number. Use π = 3.14.

   Ⓐ 24 cm
   Ⓑ 10 cm
   Ⓒ 20 cm
   Ⓓ 19 cm

4. What is the area of a circle with a diameter of 24in.?

   Use 3.14 for pi. Round to the nearest whole number if needed.

5. Which of the following adverbs fits best in the blank in this sentence?

My uncle's computer which was made in 1987 connects _____ to the Internet.

Ⓐ angrily
Ⓑ slowly
Ⓒ quickly
Ⓓ fast

6. What piece of punctuation should always appear between two coordinate adjectives?

Ⓐ A semi-colon
Ⓑ A comma
Ⓒ A period
Ⓓ A colon

7. What part of speech is the underlined word in the following sentence?

After a long, drawn out argument, the girl and her mother hugged for a long time and decided the girl's curfew was <u>hardly</u> worth fighting about.

Ⓐ Adverb
Ⓑ Adjective
Ⓒ Noun
Ⓓ Verb

8. What part of speech is the underlined word?

Sandra was worried she did not do well on her algebra test.

DAY 4

CHALLENGE YOURSELF!

✔ Circles
✔ Managing Modifiers

🌐 www.lumoslearning.com/a/dc7-24

See the first page
for Signup details

1. **Find x.**

Ⓐ 40°
Ⓑ 60°
Ⓒ 80°
Ⓓ 100°

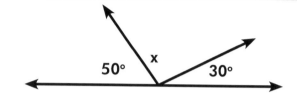

2. **Find the measures of the missing angles in the figure below.**

Ⓐ 30° and 60°
Ⓑ 60° and 90°
Ⓒ 50° and 100°
Ⓓ 60° and 120°

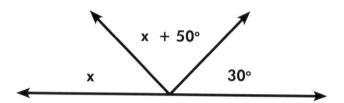

3. **The sum of the measures of angles a and b is 155 degrees. What is the measure of angle b?**

Ⓐ 155 degrees
Ⓑ 77.5 degrees
Ⓒ 35 degrees
Ⓓ 210.5 degrees

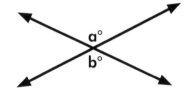

4. **If the sum of the measures of angles a and b is 240 degrees, what is the measure of angle c?**

Ⓐ 60 degrees
Ⓑ 30 degrees
Ⓒ 160 degrees
Ⓓ 150 degrees

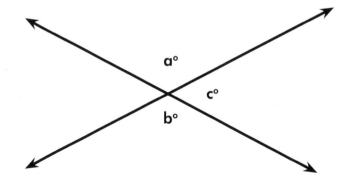

5. Where should a comma be placed in the following sentence?

The fascinating intelligent old man told us all about his experiences during the war.

(A) fascinating, intelligent
(B) intelligent, old
(C) experiences, during
(D) the, fascinating

6. Which choice best combines the following sentences with coordinate adjectives?

Slippery roads are common during the winter.
Slippery roads are also dangerous roads.

(A) Slippery and dangerous roads are common during the winter.
(B) Slippery, dangerous roads are common during the winter.
(C) Slippery, and also dangerous, roads are common during the winter.
(D) Slippery roads are common during the winter and are dangerous.

7. Which sentence contains coordinate adjectives?

(A) The loud African parrot squawked at me.
(B) Angry, frustrated customers stormed the store.
(C) The sleepy little baby rubbed his eyes.
(D) Adorable baby jaguars ran around at the zoo.

8. Which choice correctly combines the two sentences using coordinate adjectives? Circle the correct answer choice.

My dog lived a long life.
My dog lived a happy life.

(A) My dog lived a long, happy life.
(B) My dog lived a long happy life.
(C) My dog lived a long life and it was happy.
(D) My dog lived a long life and a happy life.

DAY
5

CHALLENGE YOURSELF!
✓ Angles
✓ Using Coordinate Adjectives!
🌐 www.lumoslearning.com/a/dc7-25

See the first page
for Signup details

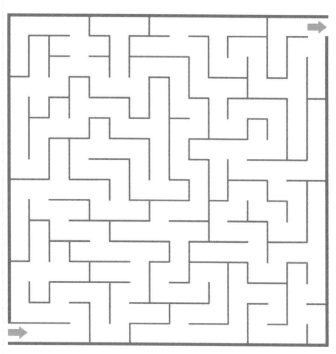

Help the beautiful kite fly out of the maze.

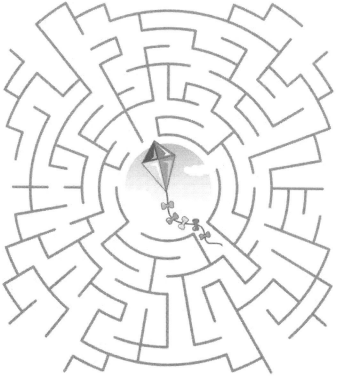

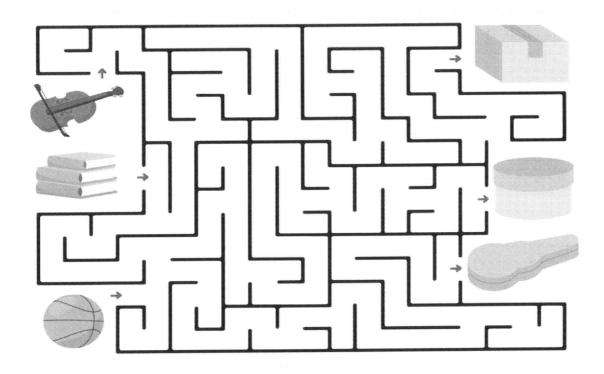

THIS WEEK'S ONLINE ACTIVITIES

✓ Reading Assignment ✓ Vocabulary Practice
✓ Write Your Summer Diary

www.lumoslearning.com/a/slh7-8

See the first page
for Signup details

WEEKLY FUN SUMMER PHOTO CONTEST

Take a picture of your summer fun activity and share it on Twitter or Instagram

Use the #SummerLearning mention

@LumosLearning on
Twitter

@lumos.learning on
Instagram

Tag friends and increase your chances of winning the contest.

PARTICIPATE AND STAND A CHANCE TO WIN $50 AMAZON GIFT CARD!

1. **Find the area of the rectangle shown below.**

6.3 cm

4.3 cm

Ⓐ 10.5 square centimeters
Ⓑ 24 square centimeters
Ⓒ 27.09 square centimeters
Ⓓ 21 square centimeters

2. **What is the volume of a cube whose sides measure 8 inches?**

Ⓐ 24 in^3
Ⓑ 64 in^3
Ⓒ 128 in^3
Ⓓ 512 in^3

3. **Calculate the area of the following polygon.**

Ⓐ 15 square units
Ⓑ 30 square units
Ⓒ 36 square units
Ⓓ 18 square units

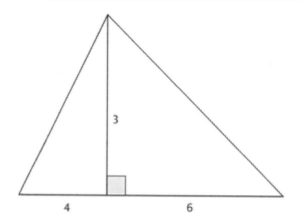

4. **What is the volume of a rectangular prism with dimensions 6, $\frac{1}{2}$, $\frac{1}{4}$ feet?**

5. Which word in the following sentence is misspelled?

We all go threw difficult times in our lives when we feel sad and lonely.

Ⓐ threw
Ⓑ difficult
Ⓒ lives
Ⓓ lonely

6. Which of the following word is misspelled?

Ⓐ Fierce
Ⓑ Sleigh
Ⓒ Experement
Ⓓ Weird

7. Which word is misspelled in the following sentence?

My favorite meal at the restaraunt is pasta with mushrooms and broccoli.

Ⓐ favorite
Ⓑ restaraunt
Ⓒ mushrooms
Ⓓ broccoli

8. Which word in this sentence is spelled incorrectly?

After I made chicken for dinner, my husband told me he prefered beef with his meals.
Write your answer in the box below.

DAY 1 CHALLENGE YOURSELF!
✔ Finding Area, Volume, & Surface Area
✔ Spellcheck!
🌐 www.lumoslearning.com/a/dc7-26

See the first page
for Signup details

1. **Joe and Mary want to calculate the average height of students in their school. Which of the following groups of students would produce the least amount of bias?**

   Ⓐ Every student in the 8th grade.
   Ⓑ Every student on the school basketball team.
   Ⓒ A randomly selected group of students in the halls.
   Ⓓ Joe & Mary's friends.

2. **Which of the following represents who you should survey in a population?**

   Ⓐ A random, representative group from the population
   Ⓑ Every individual in a population
   Ⓒ Only those in the population that agree with you
   Ⓓ Anyone, including those not in the population

3. **What does increasing the sample size of a survey do for the overall results?**

   Ⓐ Decreases bias in the results
   Ⓑ Increases the mean of the results
   Ⓒ Increases the reliability of the results
   Ⓓ Increasing sample size does not impact the results of a survey

4. **A jar of marbles contains gray and black marbles. You collect the representative sample shown here:**

   If the jar contains 50 marbles, about how many marbles are gray?

   Write your answer in the box given below.

5. Which choice best rewrites the following sentence with precise, concise language?

I am having a good day.

Ⓐ I am having a great day.
Ⓑ I am having a really good day.
Ⓒ I am having an extremely productive day.
Ⓓ I am having a really, really good day.

6. Which choice uses the most precise and concise language?

Ⓐ Hunting animals, like those who are endangered, is very wrong and not okay to do.
Ⓑ Hunting animals, like those who are endangered, is very wrong.
Ⓒ Hunting endangered animals is very wrong.
Ⓓ Hunting endangered animals is illegal.

In the first line of her book report, Maria writes:
The novel I read is about a pig whose name is Wilbur and he lives on a farm.

7. Which is NOT something Maria can do to make her sentence more precise?

Ⓐ Include the title of the book instead of "the novel I read."
Ⓑ Change "whose name is" to "named"
Ⓒ Say "who lives on a farm" instead of "and he lives on a farm."
Ⓓ Add more details about Wilbur.

8. Which choice makes George's letter most precise and concise? Circle the correct answer choice.

Ⓐ I love camp. I love it because we play sports, go canoeing, and sing songs by the campfire.
Ⓑ I love camp. I love it because we play basketball and football, go canoeing, and sing songs by the campfire.
Ⓒ I love camp because we play basketball and football, go canoeing, and sing songs by the campfire.
Ⓓ I love camp because we play sports, go canoeing, and sing songs by the campfire.

DAY
2

CHALLENGE YOURSELF!
✔ Sampling a Population
✔ Precise and Concise Language

🌐 www.lumoslearning.com/a/dc7-27

See the first page
for Signup details

John comes up with the following methods for generating unbiased samples from shoppers at a mall.

I. Ask random strangers in the mall

II. Always go to the mall at the same time of day

III. Go to different places in the mall

IV. Don't ask questions the same way to different people

1. Which of these techniques represents the best way of generating an unbiased sample?

Ⓐ I and II
Ⓑ I and III
Ⓒ I, II, and III
Ⓓ All of these

2. These two samples are about students' favorite subjects. What inference can you make concerning the students' favorite subjects?

Student samples	Science	Math	English Language Arts	Total
#1	40	14	30	84
#2	43	17	33	96

Ⓐ Students prefer Science over the other subjects.
Ⓑ Students prefer Math over the other subjects.
Ⓒ Students prefer English language arts over the other subjects.
Ⓓ Students prefer History over the other subjects.

3. These two samples are about students' favorite types of movies. What inference can you make concerning the students' favorite types of movies?

Student samples	Action	Drama	Comedy	Total
#1	45	19	35	99
#2	48	22	38	108

Ⓐ Students prefer action movies over the other types.
Ⓑ Students prefer drama over the other types.
Ⓒ Students prefer comedy over the other types.
Ⓓ none

Your school is thinking about starting a drama club but they want to know if students like the idea. To sample the population, the principal is going to survey every 10th student that walks into the school on Monday morning starting with the first student.

4. Circle the method of sampling this describes.

Ⓐ Simple Random Sampling
Ⓑ Systematic Sampling
Ⓒ Convenience Sampling

Still, there was something that was bothering Sam. The tryouts for the tennis team were on the same day as his mom's birthday, and he knew his family was planning a huge surprise party for her. He didn't want to hurt his mom's feelings by missing the party, but he also didn't want to miss his one shot at being a champion tennis player just because the tryouts were on his mom's birthday. He was in a quandary; he didn't know what to do.

5. What is the meaning of the word "quandary" in the above passage?

- Ⓐ a state of elation
- Ⓑ a state of certainty
- Ⓒ a state of perplexity
- Ⓓ a simple state of mind

Hold him, everybody! In goes the hypodermic—Bruno squeals — 10 c.c. of the antidote enters his system without a drop being wasted. Ten minutes later: condition unchanged! Another 10 c.c. Injected! Ten minutes later: breathing less torturous— Bruno can move his arms and legs a little although he cannot stand yet. Thirty minutes later: Bruno gets up and has a great feed! He looks at us disdainfully, as much as to say, 'What's barium carbonate to a big black bear like me?' Bruno was still eating. I was really happy to see him recover.

6. What is the meaning of the word "hypodermic"?

- Ⓐ aortic
- Ⓑ skin
- Ⓒ orally administered drugs
- Ⓓ injection

Of all the life forms on earth, those living in the rivers, lakes, and oceans seem to be most interesting to people. We are extremely curious about these aquatic creatures. Countless movies, television shows, books and magazines focus on animals living in the water.

7. What is the meaning of the underlined word in this passage?

- Ⓐ fish
- Ⓑ blue-colored
- Ⓒ exciting
- Ⓓ living in water

In medical school students must dissect cadavers to learn about human anatomy.

8. What is a cadaver? Circle the correct answer choice.

Ⓐ A computer model
Ⓑ A frog
Ⓒ A human body
Ⓓ A criminal

DAY 3
CHALLENGE YOURSELF!
✔ Describing Multiple Samples
✔ Figuring it out with Context Clues
🌐 www.lumoslearning.com/a/dc7-28

See the first page for Signup details

1. Consider the following dot-plot for Height versus Weight.

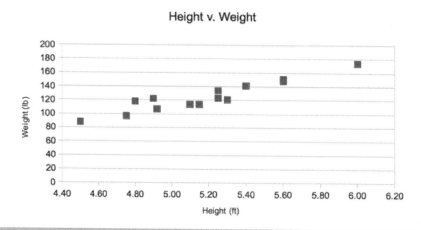

Height v. Weight

What does this dot-plot indicate about the correlation between height and weight?

Ⓐ There is no correlation.
Ⓑ There is a strong negative correlation.
Ⓒ There is a strong positive correlation.
Ⓓ There is a weak positive correlation.

2. The following chart represents the heights of boys on the basketball and soccer teams.

Basketball	Soccer
5'4"	4'11"
5'2"	4'10"
5'3"	5'9"
5'5"	5'1"
5'5"	5'0"
5'1"	5'1"
5'9"	5'3"
5'3"	5'1"

What inference can be made based on this information?

Ⓐ Soccer players have a higher average skill level than basketball players.
Ⓑ Soccer players have a lower average weight than basketball players.
Ⓒ Basketball players have a higher average height than soccer players.
Ⓓ No inference can be made.

3. Use the table below to answer the question that follows:

Month	Avg Temp.
January	24°F
February	36°F
March	55°F
April	65°F
May	72°F
June	78°F

What is difference between the mean temperature of the first four months of the year and the mean temperature of the next two months?

Ⓐ 15 degrees
Ⓑ 20 degrees
Ⓒ 25 degrees
Ⓓ 30 degrees

4. The mean of a data set is 5. The minimum of the data is 2. What is the deviation of the minimum? Write your answer in the box given below.

5. Determine the meaning of the word autonomous based on the following affixes.

Auto-=self
Nom=order
-ous=having the quality of

Ⓐ ordering something for yourself
Ⓑ being different than other people
Ⓒ having the qualities of self and order
Ⓓ being able to do something by yourself

6. The affix *path* means "to feel". What is the meaning of *empathetic* in the following sentence?

Because Mrs. Anderson is an empathetic person, she tries to help everyone in her church who is suffering.

Ⓐ nice
Ⓑ caring
Ⓒ helpful
Ⓓ cruel

Aqua-=water
Phobos=fear

7. If Juan is aquaphobic, what would be true about him?

Ⓐ He would love to go to the swimming pool.
Ⓑ He would wash the dishes after dinner each night.
Ⓒ He would avoid taking baths and showers.
Ⓓ He would want a fish as a pet.

8. A letter or group of letters added at the end of a word which makes a new word is called a _____ .

DAY 4

CHALLENGE YOURSELF!
✔ Mean, Median, and Mean Absolute Deviation
✔ Review – Roots and Affixes

🌐 www.lumoslearning.com/a/dc7-29

See the first page
for Signup details

1. **The following data set represents a score from 1-10 for a customer's experience at a local restaurant.**

    { 1, 1, 2, 1, 3, 4, 7, 8, 1, 3, 4, 2, 1, 3, 7, 2 }

    If a score of 1 means the customer did not have a good experience, and a 10 means the customer had a fantastic experience, what can you infer by looking at the data?

    Ⓐ Overall, customers had a good experience.
    Ⓑ Overall, customers had a bad experience.
    Ⓒ Overall, customers had an "ok" experience.
    Ⓓ Nothing can be inferred from this data.

2. **The manager of a local pizza place has asked you to make suggestions on how to improve his menu. The following bar graph represents the results of a survey asking customers what their favorite food at the restaurant was.**

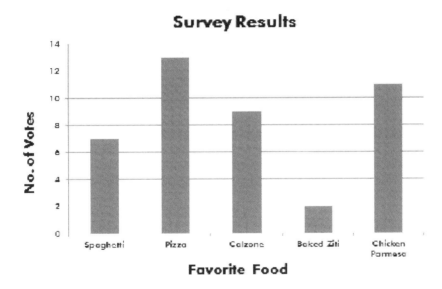

    Based on these survey results, which menu item would you suggest the manager remove from the menu?

    Ⓐ Spaghetti
    Ⓑ Pizza
    Ⓒ Calzone
    Ⓓ Baked Ziti

3. **What are the measures of central tendency?**

Ⓐ Mean, Median, Mode
Ⓑ Median, Mode, Mean Absolute Deviation
Ⓒ Median, Mean Absolute Deviation, Sample Size
Ⓓ Mean, Median, Range

4. **Find the interquartile range of the data set.**

32.6, 98.5, 16.6, 22.4, 99.8, 72.6, 68.2, 51.8, and 49.3.

While reading his science textbook, Jorge comes across the following sentence:
Animals are part of different ecosystems around the world.

5. If he wanted to find the meaning of "ecosystems," where would be the best place to look so he can find the definition quickly?

- Ⓐ In a dictionary
- Ⓑ In the glossary
- Ⓒ In a thesaurus
- Ⓓ In another chapter

While reading his science textbook, Jorge comes across the following sentence:
Animals are part of different ecosystems around the world.

6. If Jorge wanted to find words similar to the word "ecosystems" where would be the best place to look?

- Ⓐ In a dictionary
- Ⓑ In the glossary
- Ⓒ In a thesaurus
- Ⓓ In another chapter

While reading his science textbook, Jorge comes across the following sentence:
Animals are part of different ecosystems around the world.

7. Jorge decides to look up the word "ecosystem" in a dictionary. Where will he find the word?

- Ⓐ Before ecology
- Ⓑ After edifice
- Ⓒ Between ecology and edifice
- Ⓓ Between ebb and ecology

Lynn is looking for a synonym to use in her essay, so she opens the thesaurus. She looks up the following entry.

delay v. 1. Storms delayed the construction process. curb, detain, hamper, hinder, hold. 2. He delayed his admission until he got back from Europe. postpone, hold, put off, shelve. 3. Don't delay, the sale is almost over. hedge, hang back, hesitate, pause, stall

8. Lynn writes the follow sentence: "The delay caused the vendors to take back their deal." She wants to find a synonym for "delay," but this particular thesaurus entry won't help. Which choice best explains why? Circle the correct answer choice.

Ⓐ   The thesaurus entry focuses on delay as a verb, not a noun.
Ⓑ   The thesaurus entry only contains three forms of the verb delay.
Ⓒ   The thesaurus entry covers the word "delay."
Ⓓ   The thesaurus entry is not the best place to find a word, the dictionary is.

WEEK 7
SUMMER PRACTICE

DAY 1

1. Mary has 3 red marbles and 7 yellow marbles in a bag. If she were to remove 2 red and 1 yellow marbles and set them aside, what is the probability of her pulling a yellow marble as her next marble?

   Ⓐ $\dfrac{1}{6}$

   Ⓑ $\dfrac{1}{7}$

   Ⓒ $\dfrac{7}{10}$

   Ⓓ $\dfrac{6}{7}$

2. John has a deck of cards (52 cards). If John removes a number 2 card from the deck, what is the probability that he will pick a number 2 card at random?

   Ⓐ 3 out of 51
   Ⓑ 4 out of 51
   Ⓒ 26 out of 51
   Ⓓ 30 out of 51

3. Maggie has a bag of coins (8 nickels, 6 quarters, 12 dimes, 20 pennies). If she picks a coin at random, what is the probability that she will pick a quarter?

   Ⓐ 2 out of 15
   Ⓑ 3 out of 23
   Ⓒ 3 out of 50
   Ⓓ 5 out of 46

4. When one number cube is rolled, the following six outcomes are possible, {1,2,3,4,5,6}.

Identify the outcomes for each event.

Fill in the blanks given in the table with the correct outcomes.

Event	Outcome
The number cube comes up odd.	1, 3, 5
The number cube comes up even.	
The number cube comes up greater than 3.	
The number cube comes up less than or equal to 5.	

Amelia worked very hard on her Social Studies project, but there were many mistakes in the essay part of the project. Her teacher didn't want to discount the effort Amelia put into the project, so she raised her grade from a C to a B.

5. Which definition of the word discount best fits its use in the following paragraph?

- (A) take an amount of money off of a bill or a price
- (B) paying interest on a loan before the payment is due
- (C) not count
- (D) leave out or not pay attention to

Even though the seventh grade class had never taken an overnight field trip before, the principal decided to approve Mr. Juarez's request to take his students to the beach for two days to study whales.

6. Which meaning of the word approve is used in the following sentence?

- (A) talk about in a positive way
- (B) officially agree to
- (C) agree to informally
- (D) show

Because the assistant manager was the manager's subordinate, he had to work on Christmas Day while the manager had the day off to spend with her family.

7. Which definition of the word subordinate best fits its use in the following sentence?

- (A) someone in a lower position
- (B) not as important
- (C) someone who depends on someone else
- (D) not as good

After many years of studying yoga, Kelly was able to master dozens of poses.

8. What does master mean in the sentence above? Circle the correct answer choice.

- (A) An artist with great skill
- (B) One who has authority over another
- (C) To become very skilled in a performance
- (D) To overcome a fear

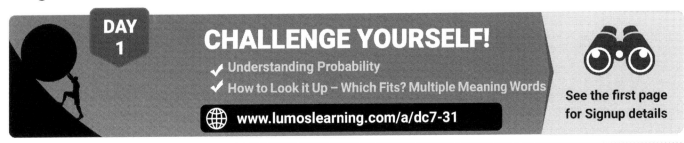

1. **Which of the following represents the sample space for flipping two coins?**

   Ⓐ {HH, TT}
   Ⓑ {H, T}
   Ⓒ {HH, HT, TH, TT}
   Ⓓ {HH, HT, TT}

2. **Which of the following experiments would best test the statement, "The probability of a coin landing on heads is 1/2."?**

   Ⓐ Toss a coin 1,000 times, and record the results.
   Ⓑ Toss a coin twice to see if it lands on heads one out of those two times.
   Ⓒ Toss a coin until it lands on heads and record the number of tries it took.
   Ⓓ Toss a coin twice, if it doesn't land on heads exactly once, the theoretical probability is false.

3. **Which of the following results is most likely from tossing a six-sided die?**

   Ⓐ Rolling an odd number
   Ⓑ Rolling an even number
   Ⓒ Rolling a number from 1 to 3
   Ⓓ All of the above are equally likely.

4. **What is the probability that the spinner will stop on the #3 sector?**

   Circle the correct answer choice.

   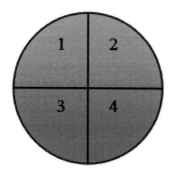

   Ⓐ 1.3

   Ⓑ $\dfrac{1}{2}$

   Ⓒ $\dfrac{1}{3}$

   Ⓓ $\dfrac{1}{4}$

As soon as Hector ate the fifteenth hotdog, he knew he had made a mistake entering the hot dog eating contest. His stomach felt <u>like a ton of bricks</u> with all that meat and bread in it!

5. What is the meaning of the underlined figure of speech?

Ⓐ light and empty
Ⓑ queasy and nauseous
Ⓒ heavy and full
Ⓓ hard and solid

Kim had spent the last three days writing the speech she was going to give the students during the assembly. She wanted more than anything to be elected as the president of the student council. When she looked down at the paper in her hand, she realized she was holding her math homework, not a copy of the speech. Kim looked up to see hundreds of pairs of eyes looking at her. Not wanting to give up on her dream of being elected and not wanting to appear unprepared, <u>Kim gave her speech off the cuff</u>.

6. What is the meaning of the underlined figure of speech?

Ⓐ quickly
Ⓑ quietly
Ⓒ embarrassedly
Ⓓ freely

Kim had spent the last three days writing the speech she was going to give the students during the assembly. She wanted more than anything to be elected as the president of the student council. When she looked down at the paper in her hand, she realized she was holding her math homework, not a copy of the speech. Kim looked up to see hundreds of pairs of eyes looking at her. Not wanting to give up on her dream of being elected and not wanting to appear unprepared, Kim gave her speech off the cuff.

7. What does the author mean by "hundreds of pairs of eyes"?

Ⓐ Many people were watching Kim carefully.
Ⓑ Many people were laughing at Kim.
Ⓒ Many people were watching Kim angrily.
Ⓓ Many people were smiling at Kim.

Robert vowed to turn over a new leaf and earn high grades in all of his classes for a change.

8. What does the underlined figure of speech mean?

    Ⓐ To commit to improving oneself
    Ⓑ To pretend to be a new person
    Ⓒ To look for ways to be different
    Ⓓ To hide one's shortcomings.

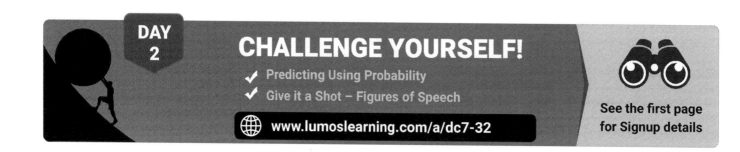

DAY 2

CHALLENGE YOURSELF!

✔ Predicting Using Probability
✔ Give it a Shot – Figures of Speech

🌐 www.lumoslearning.com/a/dc7-32

See the first page
for Signup details

1. Sara rolls two dice, one black and one yellow. What is the probability that she will roll a 3 on the black die and a 5 on the yellow die?

   Ⓐ $\dfrac{1}{6}$

   Ⓑ $\dfrac{1}{12}$

   Ⓒ $\dfrac{2}{15}$

   Ⓓ $\dfrac{1}{36}$

2. Which of the following represents the probability of an event most likely to occur?

   Ⓐ 0.25
   Ⓑ 0.91
   Ⓒ 0.58
   Ⓓ 0.15

3. Which of the following is not a valid probability?

   Ⓐ 0.25

   Ⓑ $\dfrac{1}{5}$

   Ⓒ 1

   Ⓓ $\dfrac{5}{4}$

4. You are playing a game using this spinner. You get one spin on each turn. Which list shows a complete probability model for the spinner? Circle the correct answer.

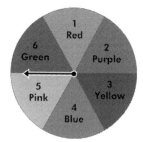

Ⓐ P(even number) = $\dfrac{3}{6}$, P(odd number) = $\dfrac{3}{6}$

Ⓑ P(red) = $\dfrac{1}{6}$, P(blue) = $\dfrac{1}{6}$

Ⓒ P(number <4) = $\dfrac{3}{6}$

Ⓓ P(yellow or green) = $\dfrac{3}{6}$, P(red or blue) = $\dfrac{3}{6}$

5. What is the relationship between the words serial and cereal?

Ⓐ They are synonyms.
Ⓑ They are antonyms.
Ⓒ They are homonyms.
Ⓓ They are opposites.

6. What is the relationship between the words annoying and unpleasant?

Ⓐ They are synonyms.
Ⓑ They are antonyms.
Ⓒ They are homonyms.
Ⓓ They are homographs.

7. Which of the following words is an antonym of the underlined word in the sentence?

Augustus enjoys <u>helping</u> others, so he volunteers at the local food bank.

Ⓐ aiding
Ⓑ entertaining
Ⓒ confusing
Ⓓ harming

By signing the document we waived our right to ask for more money at a later date. We were committed to the amount on the contract.

8. Abandon is a ____ for the word in bold above.

Ⓐ Homonym
Ⓑ Synonym
Ⓒ Antonym

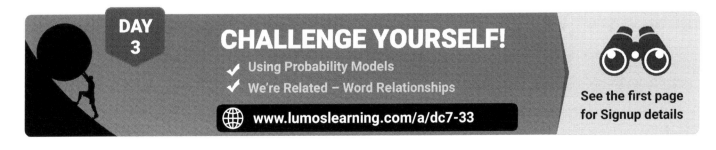

1. Felix flipped a coin 8 times and got the following results: H, H, T, H, H, T, T, H. If these results were typical for that coin, what are the odds of flipping a heads with that coin?

   Ⓐ 3 out of 5
   Ⓑ 5 out of 8
   Ⓒ 3 out of 8
   Ⓓ 1 out of 2

2. Bridgette rolled a six-sided die 100 times to test the frequency of each number's appearing. According to these statistics, how many times should a 2 be rolled out of 50 rolls?

   Ⓐ 10 times
   Ⓑ 20 times
   Ⓒ 12 times
   Ⓓ 15 times

Number	Frequency
1	18%
2	20%
3	16%
4	11%
5	18%
6	17%

3. Randomly choosing a number out of a hat 50 times resulted in choosing an odd number a total of four more times than the number of times an even number was chosen. How many times was an even number chosen from the hat?

   Ⓐ 27 times
   Ⓑ 21 times
   Ⓒ 29 times
   Ⓓ 23 times

4. The table shows observed frequencies of rolling a six sided dice. Mark the probabilities of different outcomes given in the table.

	Experiment Table						
Outcome	1	2	3	4	5	6	50 total
Frequency	7	9	10	8	9	7	trials

	$\frac{24}{50}$	$\frac{26}{50}$
Probability of rolling greater than or equal to 4		
Probability of rolling less than 4		
Probability of rolling an even number		
Probability of rolling an odd number		

Omar is always making jokes and trying to get others to laugh. Even when a situation is serious, he tries to make light of it by joking. When Omar told his friends that his grandmother was very sick and might die, everyone thought he was just joking around. Omar was trying to share something very sad, but his friends thought he was being <u>facetious</u>.

5. The denotation of facetious is "amusing or funny". Based on the context of its use in this paragraph, what is the connotation of the word?

Ⓐ positive
Ⓑ negative

Selma is often late to work, and when she does arrive there, she is lazy and rude to the customers. Selma's boss, Nick, met with her to talk with her about her job performance. Nick said Selma has many good qualities, but he needs to <u>boot</u> her from her job immediately.
The word *boot* means "to end someone's employment."

6. Based on this paragraph, the connotation of this word is...

Ⓐ negative
Ⓑ positive
Ⓒ neutral

The manager of the sandwich shop takes home the leftover rolls and bread each night to feed his children and his wife. He does this because his family is <u>needy</u>.

7. If the underlined word was changed to greedy, how would the connotation of the sentence change?

Ⓐ The reader would think of the manager as someone who wants, but does not need the leftovers.
Ⓑ The reader would think of the manager as someone who needs, but does not want the leftovers.
Ⓒ The reader's view of the manager will not change because the connotation of both words is the same.

Mother spent the afternoon talking to our nosy neighbor, Mrs. Jones.

8. What word would change the connotation of this sentence to neutral. Circle the correct answer choice.

   Ⓐ Interested
   Ⓑ Talkative
   Ⓒ Chatty
   Ⓓ Annoying

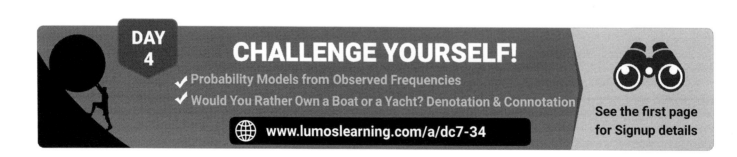

DAY 4

CHALLENGE YOURSELF!

✔ Probability Models from Observed Frequencies
✔ Would You Rather Own a Boat or a Yacht? Denotation & Connotation

🌐 www.lumoslearning.com/a/dc7-34

See the first page
for Signup details

1. The following tree diagram represents Jane's possible outfits:

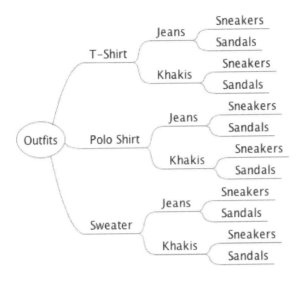

How many different outfits can Jane make based on this diagram?

Ⓐ 2
Ⓑ 12
Ⓒ 16
Ⓓ 4

2. The following tree diagram represents Jane's possible outfits:

Ⓐ $\dfrac{1}{12}$

Ⓑ $\dfrac{1}{3}$

Ⓒ $\dfrac{1}{4}$

Ⓓ $\dfrac{1}{2}$

3. Paul, Jack, Tom, Fred, and Sam are competing in the long jump. If they win the top five spots, how many ways could they be arranged in the top five spots?

Ⓐ 15 ways
Ⓑ 60 ways
Ⓒ 120 ways
Ⓓ 3,125 ways

4. A jar is filled with 4 blue marbles, 2 yellow marbles, 5 red marbles, and 3 white marbles. Two marbles are chosen at random (one at a time) from the jar. What is the probability that a red marble and then a blue marble are chosen?

Write the answer in the box. Reduce the fraction to its simplest form and write it in the box given below.

"Bruno the Bear"
Excerpt from The Bond of Love

Read the story below and answer the questions that follow.

I WILL begin with Bruno, my wife's pet sloth bear. I got him for her by accident. Two years ago, we were passing through the cornfields near a small town in Iowa. People were driving away the wild pigs from the fields by shooting at them. Some were shot, and some escaped. We thought that everything was over when suddenly a black sloth bear came out panting in the hot sun. Now I will not shoot a sloth bear wantonly, but unfortunately for the poor beast, one of my companiondid not feel the same way about it and promptly shot the bear on the spot.

As we watched the fallen animal, we were surprised to see that the black fur on its back moved and left the prostrate body. Then we saw it was a baby bear that had been riding on its mother's back when the sudden shot had killed her. The little creature ran around its prostrate parent, making a pitiful noise. I ran up to it to attempt a capture. It scooted into the sugarcane field. Following it with my companions, I was at last able to grab it by the scruff of its neck while it snapped and tried to scratch me with its long, hooked claws. We put it in one of the large jute-bags we had brought, and when I got back home, I duly presented it to my wife. She was delighted! She at once put a blue colored ribbon around its neck, and after discovering the cub was a 'boy,' she christened it Bruno. Bruno soon took to drinking milk from a bottle. It was but a step further, and within a very few days, he started eating and drinking everything else. And everything is the right word, for he ate porridge made from any ingredients, vegetables, fruit, nuts, meat (especially pork), curry and rice regardless of condiments and chilies, bread, eggs, chocolates, sweets, pudding, ice-cream, etc., etc., etc. As for drink: milk, tea, coffee, lime juice, aerated water, buttermilk, beer, alcoholic liquor, and, in fact, anything liquid. It all went down with relish. The bear became very attached to our two dogs and to all the children living in and around our farm. He was left quite free in his younger days and spent his time playing, running into the kitchen, and going to sleep in our beds. One day an accident befell him. I put down poison (barium carbonate) to kill the rats and mice that had got into my library. Bruno entered the library as he often did and ate some of the poison. Paralysis set into the extent that he could not stand on his feet. But he dragged himself on his stumps to my wife, who called me. I guessed what had happened. Off I rushed him in the car to the vet's residence. A case of poisoning! Tame Bear—barium carbonate—what to do? Out came his medical books, and a feverish reference to index began: "What poison did you say, sir?" he asked, "Barium carbonate," I said. "Ah yes—B—Ba—Barium Salts—Ah! Barium carbonate! Symptoms— paralysis— treatment—injections of . ... Just a minute, sir. I'll bring my syringe and the medicine." Said the doc. I dashed back to the car. Bruno was still floundering about on his stumps, but clearly, he was weakening rapidly; there was some vomiting, he was breathing heavily, with heaving flanks and gaping mouth. I was really scared and did not know what to do. I was feeling very guilty and was running in and out of the vet's house doing everything the doc asked me.

"Hold him, everybody!" In goes the hypodermic—Bruno squeals — 10 c.c. of the antidote enters his system without a drop being wasted. Ten minutes later: condition unchanged! Another 10 c.c. Injected! Ten minutes later: breathing less torturous— Bruno can move his arms and legs a little although he cannot stand yet. Thirty minutes later: Bruno gets up and has a great feed! He looks at us disdainfully, as much as to say, 'What's barium carbonate to a big black bear like me?' Bruno was still eating. I was really happy to see him recover. The months rolled on, and Bruno had grown many times the size he was when he came. He had equaled the big dogs in height and had even outgrown them. But was just as sweet, just as mischievous, just as playful. And he was very fond of us all. Above all, he loved my wife, and she loved him too! And he could do a few tricks, too. At the command, 'Bruno, wrestle,' or 'Bruno, box,' he vigorously tackled anyone who came forward for a rough and tumble. Give him a stick and say 'Bruno, hold the gun,' and he pointed to the stick at you. Ask him, 'Bruno, where's baby?' and he immediately produced and cradled affectionately a stump of wood which he had carefully concealed in his straw bed. But because of the neighborhoods' and our renters' children, poor Bruno, had to be kept chained most of the time. Then my son and I advised my wife and friends advised her, too, to give Bruno to the zoo. He was getting too big to keep at home. After some weeks of such advice, she at last consented. Hastily, and before she could change her mind, a letter was written to the curator of the zoo. Did he want a tame bear for his collection? He replied, "Yes." The zoo sent a cage in a truck, a distance of hundred – eighty – seven miles, and Bruno was packed off. We all missed him greatly, but in a sense, we were relieved. My wife was inconsolable. She wept and fretted. For the first few days, she would not eat a thing. Then she wrote a number of letters to the curator. How was Bruno? Back came the replies, "Well, but fretting; he refuses food too." After that, friends visiting the zoo were begged to make a point of seeing how Bruno was getting along. They reported that he was well but looked very thin and sad. All the keepers at the zoo said he was fretting. For three months, I managed to restrain my wife from visiting the zoo. Then she said one day, "I must see Bruno. Either you take me by car, or I will go myself by bus or train myself." So I took her by car. Friends had conjectured that the bear would not recognize her. I had thought so too. But while she was yet some yards from his cage, Bruno saw her and recognized her. He howled with happiness. She ran up to him, petted him through the bars, and he stood on his head in delight. For the next three hours, she would not leave that cage. She gave him tea, lemonade, cakes, ice cream, and whatnot. Then 'closing time' came and we had to leave. My wife cried bitterly; Bruno cried bitterly; even the hardened curator and the keepers felt depressed. As for me, I had reconciled myself to what I knew was going to happen next.

Oh please, sir," she asked the curator, "may I have my Bruno back"? Hesitantly, he answered, "Madam, he belongs to the zoo and is Government property now. I cannot give away Government property. But if my boss, the superintendent, agrees, certainly, you may have him back." There followed the return journey home and a visit to the superintendent's office. A tearful pleading: "Bruno and I are both fretting for each other. Will you please give him back to me?" He was a kind-hearted man and consented. Not only that, but he wrote to the curator, telling him to lend us a cage for transporting the bear back home. Back we went to the zoo again, armed with the superintendent's letter. Bruno was driven into a small cage and hoisted on top of the car; the cage was tied securely, and a slow and careful return journey back home was accomplished. Once home, a squad of workers were engaged for special work around our yard. An island was made for Bruno. It was twenty feet long and fifteen feet wide and was surrounded by a dry moat, six feet wide and seven feet deep. A wooden box that once housed fowls was brought and put on the island for Bruno to sleep in at night. Straw was placed inside to keep him warm, and his 'baby,' the gnarled stump, along with his 'gun,' the piece of bamboo, both of which had been sentimentally preserved since he had been sent away to the zoo, were put back for him to play with. In a few days, the workers hoisted the cage on to the island, and Bruno was released. He was delighted; standing on his hind legs, he pointed his 'gun' and cradled his 'baby.' My wife spent hours sitting on a chair there while he sat on her lap. He was fifteen months old and pretty heavy too! The way my wife reaches the island and leaves it is interesting. I have tied a rope to the overhanging branch of a maple tree with a loop at its end. Putting one foot in the loop, she kicks off with the other, to bridge the six-foot gap that constitutes the width of the surrounding moat. The return journey back is made the same way. But who can say now that a sloth bear has no sense of affection, no memory, and no individual characteristics?

5. Which word from the passage describes "a keeper or custodian of a collection"?

Ⓐ superintendent
Ⓑ squad
Ⓒ curator
Ⓓ worker

6. Which word from the passage describes "a high-ranking official" or "someone who manages an organization"?

Ⓐ superintendent
Ⓑ squad
Ⓒ curator
Ⓓ worker

7. Which word from the passage describes "a group of people assembled to complete a task"?

Ⓐ property
Ⓑ squad
Ⓒ curator
Ⓓ workers

Bushmen

Read the information below and answer the questions that follow.

With so much technology around us each day, it is hard to imagine that anyone in the world would live without television, let alone a cell phone or radio. Still, there are a few cultures that maintain an extremely primitive lifestyle, nearly untouched by the modern world. One of those is commonly known as the Bushmen of Kalahari.

The Bushmen, also known as the "Basarwa" or "San" is found throughout southern Africa in regions of the Kalahari Desert. Nomadic hunters and gatherers by nature, they roam the region living in small kinship groups and, relatively isolated from the rest of society, have developed an extremely unique culture not otherwise seen or understood by modern man.

Unlike English, which is built on a complex system of sounds and letters, the Bushmen speak an extremely unique language made exclusively of clicking sounds. The sounds are created with a sucking action from the tongue, and even the click language itself can vary widely from tribe to tribe, making it extremely difficult to communicate with non-Bush people.

In addition to language, the Bushmen have a very different way of living. Similar to Eskimos, groups of Bushmen will live in "kinship" societies. Led by their elders, they travel together, with women in the group gathering food while men hunt for it. Children, on the other hand, have no duties other than playing. In fact, lei-sure is an extremely important part of Bush-men society. Dance, music, and humor are essential, with a focus on family rather than technology or development. Because of this, some people associate the Bush culture with a backward kind of living or low status.

Because of the increased speed of advancement and urban development, the Bushmen culture is in danger. Some have already been forced to switch from hunting to farming due to modernization programs in their countries. Others have been forced to move to certain areas of their countries so that modernization can continue to occur there. With so much development, it's clear that though the Bushmen culture is very rich, it is also in danger of extinction. It is unclear how long the Bush culture will continue.

8. Based on the passage, what is the best meaning of primitive?

Ⓐ New and modern
Ⓑ Not sophisticated or developed
Ⓒ Cultural traits or traditions
Ⓓ Languages unlike English

UNDERWATER WORLD

Puzzle 1 Grid:

S	S	H	A	S	H	C	R	A	B
T	I	S	R	K	E	L	L	N	A
G	N	E	A	H	O	D	O	C	E
R	A	Y	L	O	R	O	L	P	H
S	Q	U	S	B	S	H	W	H	I
T	D	I	T	O	E	S	L	A	N
U	R	T	E	C	F	I	E	L	R
J	E	L	R	T	O	P	U	A	E
E	S	E	A	B	E	D	S	R	E
L	L	Y	F	I	S	H	C	O	F

Word list:
- ANEMONE
- COD
- CORAL REEF
- CRAB
- DOLPHIN
- FISH
- FLYING FISH
- HALIBUT
- HERRING
- JELLYFISH
- LOBSTER
- MORAY EEL
- MUSSEL
- OCEAN
- OCTOPUS

Words go left, right, up, down, not diagonally, and can bend at a right angle. There are no unused letters in the grid, every letter is used only once.

Word list:
- OYSTER
- PLANKTON
- SALMON
- SCUBA DIVING
- SEABED
- SEAHORSE
- SEAWEED
- SHARK
- SHELL
- SQUID
- STARFISH
- STINGRAY
- TURTLE
- URCHIN
- WHALE

Puzzle 2 Grid:

S	A	L	M	A	N	E	M	E	T
S	M	O	O	P	N	K	O	N	U
T	A	R	N	L	A	T	O	N	B
S	R	A	Y	U	R	M	L	E	I
C	F	I	E	E	C	U	S	S	L
U	B	S	H	L	H	I	N	H	A
C	A	D	I	V	O	T	E	R	D
O	D	G	N	I	Y	S	G	S	E
F	I	N	H	S	E	H	N	E	E
L	Y	G	F	I	R	R	I	A	W

ANSWER:

(answer grids shown inverted)

MERRY CHRISTMAS!

Grid 1:

S	R	E	T	W	F	L	A	P	O
T	W	I	N	O	N	S	K	H	L
H	G	I	L	S	A	M	E	T	E
S	S	S	T	F	I	T	S	R	O
T	E	B	E	C	G	S	R	E	N
N	L	A	M	E	C	I	G	E	S
E	B	U	B	D	H	R	R	T	D
M	S	R	E	S	A	N	E	I	R
A	U	A	L	C	A	T	I	N	A
N	R	O	R	E	E	D	N	G	C

Word list (top right):

- BAUBLES
- CANDY CANE
- CAROLS
- CHRISTMAS LIGHTS
- CHRISTMAS TREE
- DECEMBER
- ELVES
- GIFTS
- GINGERBREAD
- GREETING CARDS
- HOLLY

Word list (middle left):

- MISTLETOE
- NORTH POLE
- NUTCRACKER
- ORNAMENTS
- POINSETTIA
- REINDEER
- ROBIN
- SANTA CLAUS
- SNOWFLAKES
- SNOWMAN
- TOY FACTORY
- WINTER

Grid 2:

E	R	O	W	M	A	N	R	B	R
K	S	N	T	S	I	M	E	G	E
C	A	R	L	E	T	O	E	N	A
H	C	C	T	U	N	S	S	I	D
R	S	E	T	T	I	E	L	G	E
I	N	I	O	P	A	V	O	C	N
S	T	M	A	S	E	L	R	A	A
T	E	E	R	T	Y	C	A	N	C
O	A	C	T	O	R	N	I	D	Y
Y	F	Y	L	L	O	H	B	O	R

ANSWER:

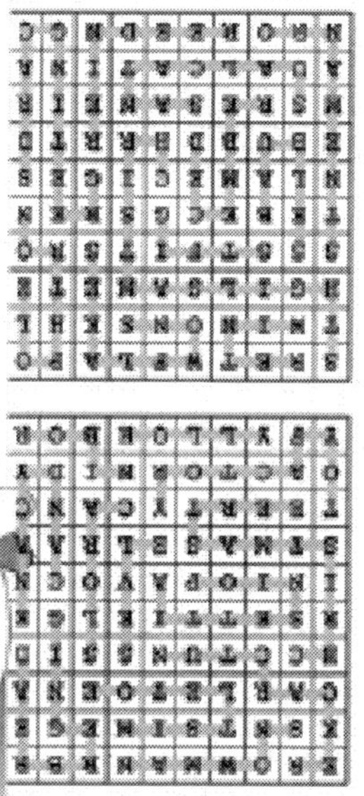

HAPPY HALLOWEEN!

Grid 1:

I	R	T	H	C	T	I	W	E	S
C	B	A	T	F	U	L	L	M	U
K	F	J	P	U	M	N	O	O	O
O	A	E	N	O	P	T	E	D	H
R	L	L	A	C	K	N	U	A	H
T	L	L	E	T	I	R	E	D	T
R	E	Y	B	O	N	S	P	I	S
C	A	O	W	B	E	R	G	H	O
H	T	R	C	E	R	A	C	S	C
I	L	D	R	E	N	Y	D	N	A

Word list:

- AUTUMN
- BAT
- BLACK CAT
- BROOMSTICK
- CANDY
- CANDY CORN
- CHILDREN
- COSTUME PARTY
- FALL
- FULL MOON
- GHOST
- HAUNTED HOUSE
- HORROW FILM

Words go left, right, up, down, not diagonally, and can bend at a right angle. There are no unused letters in the grid, every letter is used only once.

Word list 2:

- JACK-O-LANTERN
- JELLY BEAN
- MUMMY
- OCTOBER
- PUMPKIN
- SAMHAIN
- SCARE CROW
- SKELETON
- SPIDER
- SPOOKY
- TRICK OR TREAT
- VAMPIRE
- WITCH

Grid 2:

C	A	N	E	R	I	P	M	A	N
U	M	D	Y	C	O	R	N	V	O
T	E	M	U	M	C	K	O	S	T
S	P	N	B	M	A	T	L	K	E
O	A	I	L	Y	J	A	A	E	L
C	R	A	A	C	K	C	N	N	H
S	T	H	B	N	R	E	T	M	O
P	Y	M	R	M	A	U	T	U	R
O	Y	A	O	L	I	F	W	O	R
O	K	S	O	M	S	T	I	C	K

ANSWER:

[answer grids shown mirrored/inverted]

THIS WEEK'S ONLINE ACTIVITIES

✓ Reading Assignment   ✓ Vocabulary Practice

✓ Write Your Summer Diary

 www.lumoslearning.com/a/slh7-8

See the first page for Signup details

WEEKLY FUN SUMMER PHOTO CONTEST

📷 Take a picture of your summer fun activity and share it on Twitter or Instagram

Use the #SummerLearning mention

@LumosLearning on
🐦
Twitter

@lumos.learning on
📷
Instagram

👤 Tag friends and increase your chances of winning the contest.

PARTICIPATE AND STAND A CHANCE TO WIN $50 AMAZON GIFT CARD!

WEEK 8
SUMMER PRACTICE

REPRESENT SAMPLE SPACES

1. **If Robbie flips a quarter twice, what is the sample space for the possible outcomes?**

   Ⓐ HT, HH, TT, TH
   Ⓑ HT, TH
   Ⓒ HT, TT, TH
   Ⓓ HH, TT

2. **If Bret rolls a six-sided die twice, which table shows the sample space for possible outcomes?**

Ⓐ
	1	2	3	4	5	6
1	1, 1	1, 2	1, 3	1, 4	1, 5	1, 6
2	2, 1	2, 2	2, 3	2, 4	2, 5	2, 6
3	3, 1	3, 2	3, 3	3, 4	3, 5	3, 6
4	4, 1	4, 2	4, 3	4, 4	4, 5	4, 6
5	5, 1	5, 2	5, 3	5, 4	5, 5	5, 6
6	6, 1	6, 2	6, 3	6, 4	6, 5	6, 6

Ⓒ
	1	2	3	4	5	6
1		1, 2	1, 3	1, 4	1, 5	1, 6
2	2, 1		2, 3	2, 4	2, 5	2, 6
3	3, 1	3, 2		3, 4	3, 5	3, 6
4	4, 1	4, 2	4, 3		4, 5	4, 6
5	5, 1	5, 2	5, 3	5, 4		5, 6
6	6, 1	6, 2	6, 3	6, 4	6, 5	

Ⓑ
	1	2	3	4	5	6
1	1, 1					
2		2, 2				
3			3, 3			
4				4, 4		
5					5, 5	
6						6, 6

Ⓓ
	1	2	3	4
1	1, 1	1, 2	1, 3	1, 4
2	2, 1	2, 2	2, 3	2, 4
3	3, 1	3, 2	3, 3	3, 4
4	4, 1	4, 2	4, 3	4, 4
5	5, 1	5, 2	5, 3	5, 4
6	6, 1	6, 2	6, 3	6, 4

3. There are three colors of stones in a bag: red, green, and blue. Two stones are drawn out at random (one at a time). What are the possible outcomes in which exactly one blue stone might be drawn?

Ⓐ BR, GB BG
Ⓑ BG, BR, BB
Ⓒ RB, GB, BR, BG
Ⓓ BG, BR

4. A bag contains red and blue marbles. In a representative sample of 10 marbles, there are 4 red marbles. Write the correct number of marbles into the blanks in the table.

	No. of Red Marbles	No. of Blue Marbles
If the bag has 100 marbles, estimate the number of red marbles and blue marbles in the bag.		
If the bag has 200 marbles, estimate the number of red marbles and blue marbles in the bag.		

Fairy Tales by A Brothers' Grimm

Read the story below and answer the questions that follow.

A certain king once fell ill, and the doctor declared that only a sudden fright would restore him to health, but the king was not a man for anyone to play tricks on, except his fool. One day, when the fool was with him in his boat, he cleverly pushed the king into the water. Help had already been arranged, and the king was drawn ashore and put to bed. The fright, the bath, and the rest in bed cured the diseased king.

The king wanted to frighten the fool for his act, so he told him that he would be put to death. He directed the executioner privately not to use the axe but to let fall a single drop of water on the fool's neck. Amidst shouts and laughter, the fool was asked to rise and thank the king for his kindness. But the fool never moved; he was dead; killed by the master's joke.

5. What trick did the fool plan to cure the king?

Ⓐ a lot of medicines
Ⓑ injections
Ⓒ the sudden push into the water
Ⓓ the ride in the boat

From "The Owl and the Pussy-Cat" by Edward Lear

Read the poem below and answer the questions that follow.

The Owl and the Pussy-Cat went to sea
 In a beautiful pea-green boat,
They took some honey, and plenty of money
 Wrapped up in a five-pound note.
The Owl looked up to the stars above,
 And sang to a small guitar,
O lovely Pussy! O Pussy, my love,
 What a beautiful Pussy you are,
  You are,
  You are!

What a beautiful Pussy you are!"
Pussy said to the Owl, "You elegant fowl!
 How charmingly sweet you sing!
O let us be married! too long we have tarried:
 But what shall we do for a ring?"
They sailed away for a year and a day,
 To the land where the Bong-tree grows,
And there in a wood a Piggy-wig stood,
 With a ring at the end of his nose,
  His nose,
  His nose,
With a ring at the end of his nose.

6. Who provides the wedding ring for the wedding?

Ⓐ The Owl
Ⓑ The Pussy-Cat
Ⓒ The Pig
Ⓓ The Bong-tree

"The Boys and the Frogs"
From Aesop's Fables, adapted by Marmaduke Park

Read the poem below and answer the questions that follow.

Someboys, beside a pond or lake,
Were playing once at duck and drake?
When, doubtless to their heart's content,
Volleys of stones were quickly sent.
But there were some (there will be such)
Who did not seem amused so much;
These were the frogs, to whom the game,
In point of sport was not the same.

For scarce a stone arrived, 'tis said,
But gave some frog a broken head;
And scores in less than half an hour,
Perished beneath the dreadful shower.
At last, said one, "You silly folks, I say,
Do fling your stones another way;
Though sport to you, to throw them thus,
Remember, pray, 'tis death to us!"

7. Part A
Why does the frog scold the boys?

Ⓐ The boys hit the frog in the head with a rock.
Ⓑ The boys are polluting the pond that the frog lives in.
Ⓒ The boys refuse to let the frog play with them.
Ⓓ The boys are trying to catch the frog to keep as a pet.

Part B
According to this poem what are the boys doing at the pond?

Ⓐ Trying to catch fish
Ⓑ Trying to catch frogs
Ⓒ Killing frogs
Ⓓ Throwing stones into the pond

The Use of Transitions

Read the poem below and answer the questions that follow.

(1)The wind was blowing with the gale force of over 55 miles an hour. (2) The windows of the house began to shake as we silently waited for the worst of all possible storms. (3) Kitchen plates crashed to the floor, and we trembled with fear.

(4)My trusty dog was by my side, and my little brother huddled under the table. (5) Our parents had gone to a neighbor's house for a community meeting. (6) This storm was not predicted by the weatherman earlier on TV. (7) We knew nothing of the impending danger.

(8)Within moments, the tornado warning sounded from the fire station downtown. (9) I grabbed my brother, Danny, and headed straight for the hallway. (10) On the way, I remembered to pull the mattress off of his bed. (11) We fell to the floor, pulled the mattress on top of us, and the faint sound of a train whistle began. (12) Suddenly it was as loud as if we were crossing the tracks. (13) Yes, my greatest fear was realized. (14) We were on the path of a pop-up tornado!

(15)Then as quickly as it began, silence. (16) No more wind, I thought to myself. (17) Boy, was I wrong! (18) Extremely loud crashing and banging of pane glass windows surrounded us. (19)The tornado was on top of us.

(20)Moments later, a gentle breeze came down the hall. (21) The calm after the storm, yes, that phrase fit. (22) I quickly checked Danny, who was underneath me. (23) He was as white as a sheet but grunted that he was ok. (24)Sapphire was fine, as well. (25) Not so for our living room, kitchen, and bedrooms. (26) The wind force had blown out all windows and lifted our roof to the street

(27)We just sat there in the hallway after checking the house and began to cry.

(28)Within moments the fire trucks were coming down our street. (29) Their megaphone was on and announcing an all clear. (30)They wanted everyone who could to come outside.

(31)My brother and I went out slowly and carefully to avoid the glass fragments. (32) Our dog followed yelping all the way. (33) Our parents were running down the street, fearing for what had happened. (34) Ours was the only house touched by the tornado! (35) Debris was everywhere. (36) Praises to the man up above, we were safe.

(37)Family and life are more important than personal belongings. (38) That I can say.

---

8. Given the information in the selection, a substantiated critique of this selection would best read as follows. Circle the correct answer choice.

Ⓐ   The author notes that tornados are frightening and can cause damage.
Ⓑ   The author makes valid statements to back up his/her account of a damaging tornado that destroyed property but not lives.
Ⓒ   The author fabricates the information and does not give supportive evidence to back up the selection.
Ⓓ   The author gave limited information in regards to the tornado damage and its impact on his/ her family's survival.

1. If 20% of applicants for a job are female, what is the probability that the first two applicants will be male?

   Ⓐ 64%
   Ⓑ 80%
   Ⓒ 60%
   Ⓓ 52%

2. If you want to simulate a random selection from a large population that is 40% adult and 60% children, how can you use slips of paper to do so?

   Ⓐ Make 5 slips of paper, 2 for adults and 3 for children. Randomly select slips of paper from the 5 to represent the choice of someone from the population.
   Ⓑ Make 2 slips of paper, 1 for adults and 1 for children. Randomly select slips of paper from the 2 to represent the choice of someone from the population.
   Ⓒ Make 100 slips of paper, 50 for adults and 50 for children. Randomly select slips of paper from the 100 to represent the choice of someone from the population.
   Ⓓ Make 3 slips of paper, 1 for adults and 2 for children. Randomly select slips of paper from the 3 to represent the choice of someone from the population.

3. A sandwich shop has 6 breads and 5 meats available for sandwiches. What is the probability that two people in a row will choose the same combination of bread and meat?

   Ⓐ 1 out of 11
   Ⓑ 1 out of 2
   Ⓒ 1 out of 30
   Ⓓ 1 out of 20

4. Suppose that for every birth of a baby the probability of a "boy" birth is 0.5 and the probability of a "girl" birth is also 0.5. Calculate the probabilities of having each of the situations described.

	0.125	0.375
Three boys	○	○
Two boys and a girl	○	○
Two girls and a boy	○	○
Three girls	○	○

From "The Dog and the Wolf" by Marmaduke Park

Read the poem below and answer the questions that follow.

A wolf there was, whose scanty fare
Had made his person lean and spare;
A dog there was, so amply fed,
His sides were plump and sleek; 'tis said
The wolf once met this prosp'rous cur,
And thus began: "Your servant, sir;
I'm pleased to see you look so well,
Though how it is I cannot tell;
I have not broke my fast to-day;
Nor have I, I'm concern'd to say,
One bone in store or expectation,
And that I call a great vexation."

5. Which of the following can be inferred about the dog based on this passage?

Ⓐ That the dog was a golden retriever
Ⓑ That the dog had a caring master
Ⓒ That the dog was tall
Ⓓ That the dog belonged to the king

"The Boys and the Frogs" by Marmaduke Park

Read the poem below and answer the questions that follow.

Someboys, beside a pond or lake,
Were playing once at duck and drake?
When, doubtless to their heart's content,
Volleys of stones were quickly sent.
But there were some (there will be such)
Who did not seem amused so much;
These were the frogs, to whom the game,
In point of sport was not the same.
For scarce a stone arrived, 'tis said,
But gave some frog a broken head;
And scores in less than half an hour,
Perished beneath the dreadful shower.
At last, said one, "You silly folks, I say,
Do fling your stones another way;
Though sport to you, to throw them thus,
Remember, pray, 'tis death to us!"

6. What is most likely true about the boys in this poem? Circle the correct answer choice.

Ⓐ They dislike frogs and want to hurt them.
Ⓑ They did not realize that the rocks would harm the frogs.
Ⓒ They want to catch the frogs to keep as pets.
Ⓓ They like rocks more than they like frogs.

From The Children of France by Ruth Royce

Read the story below and answer the questions that follow.

Before the "Squire's" son went away to war, the neighborhood children knew him only by sight and by hearing their parents speak of him as the son of "the richest man in Titusville," who never had done a day's work in his life.

Perhaps the parents were not quite right in this, for, even if Robert Favor had not gone out in the fields to labor, he had graduated from high school and college with high honors. He never spoke to the village children nor noticed them, and was not, as a result, very popular with the young people of his home town. The neighbors said this was all on account of his bringing up.

It was therefore a surprise to them when, at the beginning of the great war, after Germany swept over Belgium, Robert Favor hurried to Europe. It was later learned that he had joined what is known as the "Foreign Legion" of the French Army. Titusville next heard that he had been made a lieutenant for heroic conduct under fire. But Titusville did not believe it; it said no Favor ever did anything but run away in such circumstances. But they believed it when, later on, they read in the newspapers howLieutenant Favor had sprung out of the trenches and ran to the rescue of a wounded private soldier who had lain in a shell hole in No Man's Land since the night before.

The village swelled with pride and the eyes of the children grew wide with wonder as they listened to the story of the heroism of the Squire's son. But this was as nothing to what occurred later. "Bob" Favor was brought home one day to the house on the hill, pale and weak from wounds received in battle.

Spring was at hand, and as soon as he was able, Captain Favor—you see he had again been promoted—was taken out on the lawn where, in his wheel chair he rested in the warm sunshine. The bright red top of his gray-blue cap, and the flash of the medal on his breast excited the wonder of the children, who pressed their faces against the high iron fence and gazed in awe. It was the first real hero any of them ever had seen.

Finally, chancing to look their way, the Captain smiled and waved a friendly hand. A little girl clapped her hands, others started to cheer and a little man of ten dragged an American flag from his pocket and waved it. The Captain beckoned to the children.

"Come in, folks," he called. "I wish someone to talk to me and make me laugh. Are you coming?"
They were. The children started, at first hesitatingly, then with more confidence, led by the boy with the American flag, which he was waving bravely now.

"What's your name?" demanded the Captain. "Joe Funk, sir."

The Captain laughed. "No boy so patriotic as you are should have a name like that," he said. "We all are going to be great friends, I am sure, and when I get this leg, that a German shell nearly blew off, in working order again, we shall have some real sport and I'll teach you all how to be soldiers. Just now I cannot do much of anything."

"Yes, you can," interrupted Joe. "You can tell us how you rescued the soldier when the Germans were shooting at you and—"
"Master Joseph," answered the Captain gravely, "a real soldier never brags about himself;

but what you say does give me an idea. How would you like to have me tell you about the brave little children of France?"

"Well, I'd rather hear about how you killed the Germans, lots of 'em; I want to hear about battles and dead men and—"

"We shall speak of the children first, and I will begin right now. Let me see. Ah! I have it. Sit down on the grass, all of you, and be comfortable. Be quiet until I finish the story, then ask what questions you wish. Now listen!"

---

7. Based on the details in this story, what do you think brought the Captain back to Titusville? Circle the correct answer choice.

Ⓐ He was injured during the war and could no longer fight.
Ⓑ He wanted to tell the people of Titusville his heroic stories.
Ⓒ He wanted to make the people of Titusville proud of him.
Ⓓ He wanted to work on his father's farm again.

From Scouting for Boys

Read the story below and answer the questions that follow.

"Hi! Stop Thief!" shouted old Blenkinsopp as he rushed out of his little store near the village.
"He's stolen my sugar. Stop him."

Stop whom? There was nobody in sight running away, ""Who stole it?"" asked the policeman.

""I don't know, but a whole bag of sugar is missing. It was there only a few minutes ago."" The policeman tried to track the thief, but it looked a pretty impossible job for him to single out the tracks of the thief from among dozens of other footprints about the store. However, he presently started off hopefully, at a jog-trot, away out into the bush. In some places, he went over the hard stony ground,

but he never checked his pace, although no footmarks could be seen. People wondered how he could possibly find the trail. Still, he trotted on. Old Blenkinsopp was feeling the heat and the pace.

At length, he suddenly stopped and cast around, having evidently lost the trail. Then a grin came on his face as he pointed with his thumb over his shoulder up the tree near which he was standing. There, concealed among the branches, they saw a young man with the missing bag of sugar.

How had the policeman spotted him? His sharp eyes had described some grains of sugar sparkling in the dust. The bag leaked, leaving a slight trail of these grains. He followed that trail, and when it came to an end in the bush, he noticed a string of ants going up a tree. They were after the sugar, and so was he, and between them, they brought about the capture of the thief.

Old Blenkinsopp was so pleased that he promptly opened the bag and spilled a lot of the sugar on the ground as a reward to the ants.

He also appreciated the policeman for his cleverness in using his eyes to see the grains of sugar and the ants, and in using his wits to know why the ants were climbing the tree."

8. The details of this story show that no one is present at the scene. Who is likely the narrator of this selection?

Ⓐ the shopkeeper
Ⓑ the narrator
Ⓒ the people
Ⓓ the thief

DAY 2

CHALLENGE YOURSELF!
✓ Simulate Compound Events to Estimate Probability
✓ Use Those Clues – Make an Inference

🌐 www.lumoslearning.com/a/dc7-37

See the first page for Signup details

1. One third of a quart of paint covers one fourth of a basketball court. How much paint does it take to paint the entire basketball court?

   Ⓐ one and one-third quarts
   Ⓑ one quart
   Ⓒ one and one-fourth quarts
   Ⓓ one and three-fourths quarts

2. The total cost of 100 pencils purchased at a constant rate is $39.00. What is the unit price?

   Ⓐ $39.00
   Ⓑ $3.90
   Ⓒ $0.39
   Ⓓ $0.039

3. A construction worker was covering the bathroom wall with tiles. He covered three-fifths of the wall with 50 tiles. How many tiles will it take to cover the entire wall?

   Ⓐ 83 tiles
   Ⓑ 83 and one-third tiles
   Ⓒ 85 tiles
   Ⓓ 83 and one-half tiles

4. Read each sentence and select whether the rate is a rate or unit rate.

	Rate	Unit Rate
The earth rotates 1.25 degrees in 5 minutes.		
Sarah reads 13 pages in 1/3 of an hour.		
A man pays $45.24 for 16 gallons of gasoline.		
The car drives 25 miles per hour.		
The soup costs $1.23 per ounce.		
40 millimeters of rain fell in 1 minute.		

5. What type of word group is the underlined portion of the following sentence?

I need a new cell phone because my old phone <u>fell in the toilet</u>.

(A) phrase
(B) dependent clause
(C) independent clause
(D) prepositional clause

6. What type of word group is the underlined portion of the following sentence?

I need a new cell phone <u>because my old phone fell in the toilet</u>.

(A) Phrase
(B) Dependent Clause
(C) Independent Clause
(D) Complete Clause

7. What type of word group is the underlined portion of the following sentence?

The actor <u>who starred in the movie version of one of my favorite books</u> did a horrible job playing the main character.

(A) phrase
(B) dependent clause
(C) independent clause
(D) interrupter phrase

8. What type of word group is the underlined portion of the following sentence?

Good things tend to happen to you <u>when you least expect them</u>.

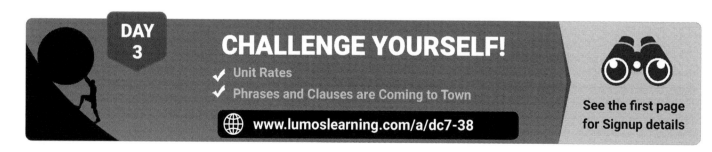

DAY
3

CHALLENGE YOURSELF!

✓ Unit Rates
✓ Phrases and Clauses are Coming to Town

🌐 www.lumoslearning.com/a/dc7-38

See the first page
for Signup details

1. The following table shows two variables in a proportional relationship:

c	d
4	8
5	10
6	12

If c and d are proportional, then d = kc where k is the constant of proportionality.

Which of the following represents k in this case?

Ⓐ k = 1
Ⓑ k = 2
Ⓒ k = 3
Ⓓ k = 4

2. **Ricky's family wants to invite his classroom to a "get acquainted" party. If 20 students attend, the party will cost $100. Assuming the relationship between cost and guests is proportional, which of the following will be the cost if 29 students attend?**

Ⓐ $129
Ⓑ $135
Ⓒ $139
Ⓓ $145

3. **Which of the following pairs of ratios form a proportion?**

Ⓐ 9 boys to 5 girls and 12 boys to 8 girls
Ⓑ 9 boys to 5 girls and 18 boys to 10 girls
Ⓒ 9 boys to 5 girls and 13 boys to 9 girls
Ⓓ 9 boys to 5 girls and 27 boys to 14 girls

4. **Suppose you are buying pizzas for a party. An equation that represents the cost (y) in dollars for x number of pizzas is y=18x.**

Does the equation y=18x represent a proportional relationship?
Instruction: Check all that are true

Ⓐ No, the graph of the equation does not pass through the origin.
Ⓑ Yes, the graph of the equation is a straight line
Ⓒ Yes, the graph of the equation passes through the origin.
Ⓓ No, the graph of the equation is not a straight line.

5. Which of the following sentences has correct subject-verb agreement?

Ⓐ Every one of us have a purpose in life.
Ⓑ Angela and her best friend goes out for pizza every Friday night.
Ⓒ I hope my favorite football team play well this weekend.
Ⓓ Why do my neighbors always get louder at night?

6. Which of the following verb forms correctly fills in the blank in the following sentence? Neither of my parents _____ going on vacation.

Ⓐ enjoy
Ⓑ enjoys
Ⓒ enjoying
Ⓓ are enjoying

7. Which of the following versions of the sentence has correct subject-verb agreement?

Ⓐ A positive attitude and motivation make school easier.
Ⓑ A positive attitude and motivation makes school easier.
Ⓒ A positive attitude and motivation is making school easier.
Ⓓ A positive attitude and motivation maked school easier.

8. Which version of this sentence has correct subject-verb agreement? Circle the correct answer choice.

Ⓐ Usually Sam or Alec are the referee for our intramural soccer game.
Ⓑ Usually Sam or Alec were the referee for our intramural soccer game.
Ⓒ Usually Sam or Alec is the referee for our intramural soccer game.
Ⓓ Usually Sam or Alec was the referee for our intramual soccer game.

DAY 4

CHALLENGE YOURSELF!
✔ Understanding and Representing Proportions
✔ Good Sentences are Built on Agreement

 www.lumoslearning.com/a/dc7-39

See the first page
for Signup details

1. When Frank buys three packs of pens, he knows he has 36 pens. When he buys five packs, he knows he has 60 pens. What is the constant of proportionality between the number of packs and the number of pens?

   Ⓐ 12
   Ⓑ 10
   Ⓒ 36
   Ⓓ 60

2. What is the constant of proportionality in the following equation?

   B = 1.25C

   Ⓐ 1.00
   Ⓑ 0.25
   Ⓒ 1.25
   Ⓓ 2.50

3. When Georgia buys 3 boxes of peaches, she has 40 pounds more than when she buys 1 box of peaches. How many pounds of peaches are in each box?

   Ⓐ 40
   Ⓑ 60
   Ⓒ 20
   Ⓓ 3

4. Suppose the relationship between x and y is proportional. If the constant of proportionality of y to x is 16, select possible values for y and x.

   Ⓐ x = 6 and y = 96
   Ⓑ x = 96 and y = 6
   Ⓒ x = 9 and y = 90
   Ⓓ x = 144 and y = 9

5. Select the sentence with the adjective underlined

Ⓐ Marta <u>hardly</u> knew where to find her orange sweater.
Ⓑ The large, angry dog <u>rushed</u> towards the mailman.
Ⓒ Everyone knows that <u>kind</u> words get a person better results than insults do.
Ⓓ I wanted to go to the movies this weekend, but I can't <u>afford</u> to because don't get paid until next Thursday.

6. Select the version of the sentence with the adjective underlined.

Ⓐ <u>Because</u> my alarm clock didn't go off this morning and there was traffic due to an accident on the highway, I was very late for my appointment with Dr. Huang.
Ⓑ Because my alarm clock didn't <u>go off</u> this morning and there was traffic due to an accident on the highway, I was very late for my appointment with Dr. Huang.
Ⓒ Because my alarm clock didn't go off this morning and there was <u>traffic</u> due to an accident on the highway, I was very late for my appointment with Dr. Huang.
Ⓓ Because my alarm clock didn't go off this morning and there was <u>heavy</u> traffic due to an accident on the highway, I was very late for my appointment with Dr. Huang.

7. Select the version of the sentence with the adverb underlined.

Ⓐ When Megan's <u>best</u> friend told her she no longer wanted to be friends, Megan angrily slammed down the phone smashing it to pieces.
Ⓑ When Megan's best friend told her she no longer <u>wanted</u> to be friends, Megan angrily slammed down the phone smashing it to pieces.
Ⓒ When Megan's best friend told her she no longer wanted to be friends, Megan <u>angrily</u> slammed down the phone smashing it to pieces.
Ⓓ When Megan's best friend told her she no longer wanted to be friends, Megan angrily slammed down the phone <u>smashing</u> it to pieces.

8. What part of speech is the underlined word?

Bill thought it was strange that his older brother offered to give him money for pizza. Write your answer in the box given below.

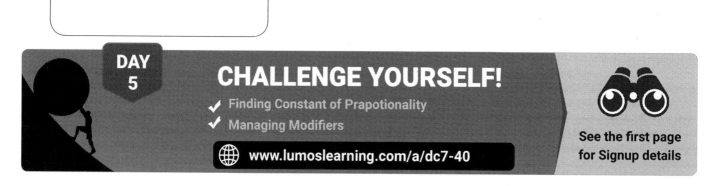

DAY 5

CHALLENGE YOURSELF!
✓ Finding Constant of Prapotionality
✓ Managing Modifiers

🌐 www.lumoslearning.com/a/dc7-40

See the first page for Signup details

THIS WEEK'S ONLINE ACTIVITIES

✔ Reading Assignment ✔ Vocabulary Practice
✔ Write Your Summer Diary

 www.lumoslearning.com/a/slh7-8

See the first page
for Signup details

WEEKLY FUN SUMMER PHOTO CONTEST

Take a picture of your summer fun activity and share it on Twitter or Instagram

Use the #SummerLearning mention

@LumosLearning on	@lumos.learning on
Twitter	**Instagram**

Tag friends and increase your chances of winning the contest.

PARTICIPATE AND STAND A CHANCE TO WIN $50 AMAZON GIFT CARD!

WEEK 9
SUMMER PRACTICE

REPRESENT PRAPARTIONS BY EQUATIONS

1. When buying bananas at the market, Marco pays $4.50 for 5 pounds. What is the relationship between pounds, p, and cost, C?

    Ⓐ   C = 4.5p
    Ⓑ   C = 5p
    Ⓒ   C = 0.9p
    Ⓓ   C = 22.5p

2. The cost to rent an apartment is proportional to the number of square feet in the apartment. An 800 square foot apartment costs $600 per month. What equation represents the relationship between area, a, and cost, C?

    Ⓐ   C = 0.75a
    Ⓑ   C = 1.33a
    Ⓒ   C = 8a
    Ⓓ   C = 6a

3. A school has to purchase new desks for their classrooms. They have to purchase 350 new desks, and they pay $7000. What equation demonstrates the relationship between the number of desks, d, and the total cost, C?

    Ⓐ   C = 10d
    Ⓑ   C = 20d
    Ⓒ   C = 70d
    Ⓓ   C = 35d

4. You run 9.1 miles in 1.3 hours at a steady rate. Write an equation that represents the proportional relationship between the x hours you run and the distance y in miles that you travel? Write the equation in the box given below

5. Which sentence uses coordinate adjectives correctly?

Ⓐ He was wearing running, black and striped shoes.
Ⓑ He was wearing black striped running shoes.
Ⓒ He was wearing black, striped running shoes.
Ⓓ He was wearing black, running striped shoes.

6. Which sentence uses coordinate adjectives incorrectly?

Ⓐ She was wearing an angora, red sweater.
Ⓑ She was wearing a comfy, fluffy angora sweater.
Ⓒ She was wearing a yellow, fluffy angora sweater.
Ⓓ She was wearing a soft, fluffy angora sweater.

7. Which sentence uses coordinate adjectives correctly?

Ⓐ He was wearing purple, rubber boots.
Ⓑ He travelled along a curvy, slippery highway.
Ⓒ He visited his aging, maternal grandmother.
Ⓓ He needs a cold, diet soda.

8. How could the following sentence be changed to use coordinating adjectives correctly?

Alisha wanted to go a tropical, warm, sunny island for Christmas.

Ⓐ Remove tropical from the sentence.
Ⓑ Move tropical after sunny and separate them with a comma.
Ⓒ Move tropical after sunny and do not add a comma.
Ⓓ Move warm before tropical.

1. At one particular store, the sale price, s, is always 75% of the displayed price, d. Which of the following equations correctly shows how to calculate s from d?

Ⓐ d = 75s
Ⓑ s = 0.75d
Ⓒ s = d - 0.75
Ⓓ s = d + 75

2. When x = 6, y = 4. If y is proportional to x, what is the value for y when x = 9?

Ⓐ 4

Ⓑ $\dfrac{2}{3}$

Ⓒ 3
Ⓓ 6

3. Jim is shopping for a suit to wear to his friend's wedding. He finds the perfect one on sale at 30% off. If the original price was $250.00, what will the selling price be after the discount?

Ⓐ $75
Ⓑ $175
Ⓒ $200
Ⓓ $220

4. Which of the expressions equals 60%? There can be more than 1 correct answer, select all the correct answers.

Ⓐ 48 of 100
Ⓑ 32.4 of 54
Ⓒ 3 of 5
Ⓓ 4 of 5
Ⓔ 32 of 53

5. Which word is misspelled in the following sentence?

I was recognised as the top spelunker at least week's cave exploration

- Ⓐ recognised
- Ⓑ spelunker
- Ⓒ exploration
- Ⓓ tournament

6. Which of the following words contains a spelling mistake?

- Ⓐ Appendix
- Ⓑ Rupture
- Ⓒ Panicked
- Ⓓ Arguing

7. Which of the following words is misspelled?

- Ⓐ Accessory
- Ⓑ Harass
- Ⓒ Necessary
- Ⓓ Possession

8. Which word in this sentence is spelled incorrectly?

Because Kay's mother is concerned about her daughter's happyness, she always does everything she can to help Kay avoid being unhappy. Write your answer in the box below.

1. Ricky purchased shoes for $159.95 and then exchanged them at a buy 1, get 1 half off sale. The shoes that he purchased on his return trip were $74.99 and $68.55. How much did he receive back from the store after his second transaction?

   Ⓐ $37.50
   Ⓑ $68.55
   Ⓒ $34.28
   Ⓓ $50.68

2. Simplify the following expression:

   $3.24 - 1.914 - 6.025 + 9.86 - 2.2 + 5\dfrac{1}{2} =$

   Ⓐ -8.461
   Ⓑ 8.461
   Ⓒ -11.259
   Ⓓ 11.259

3. John had $76.00. He gave Jim $42.45 and gave Todd $21.34. John will receive $14.50 later in the evening. How much money will John have later that night?

   Ⓐ $25.71
   Ⓑ $26.67
   Ⓒ $26.71
   Ⓓ $24.71

4. Jeri has had a savings account since she entered first grade. Each month of the first year she saved $1.00. Each month of the second year she saved $2.00 etc until she completed ten years in which she saved $10.00 each month. How much does she have saved at the end of ten years?

   Ⓐ $660
   Ⓑ $648
   Ⓒ $636
   Ⓓ $624

In the first line of her book report, Maria writes:
The novel I read is about a pig whose name is Wilbur and he lives on a farm.

5. Which choice represents the MOST precise opening line Maria could write?

Ⓐ Charlotte's Web is about a pig named Wilbur who lives on a farm.
Ⓑ The novel I read is about a pig named Wilbur and he lives on a farm.
Ⓒ The novel I read is about a pig whose name is Wilbur who lives on a farm.
Ⓓ Charlotte's Web is about a pig named Wilbur and he lives on a farm.

Alfonso is writing a restaurant review. He writes the following:
The baked goods were delicious.

6. How can Alfonso be more precise with his review?

Ⓐ Change "baked goods" to a specific baked good he tried.
Ⓑ Change "delicious" to "good".
Ⓒ Change "baked goods" to "bakery items"
Ⓓ Change "The" to the name of the restaurant.

Alfonso is writing a restaurant review. He writes the following:
The baked goods were delicious.

7. Which sentence below does NOT make Alfonso's sentence more precise?

Ⓐ The baked goods were incredibly yummy and delicious.
Ⓑ The donuts were soft and warm.
Ⓒ The chocolate chip cookies were ooey and gooey.
Ⓓ The cakes and cookies were the best I've ever had.

After seeing a play, Yuri writes the following sentence:
The actresses wore dresses.

8. Which is NOT something Yuri can do to make the sentence more precise?

Ⓐ Describe a particular actress's dress
Ⓑ Add more details about the dresses
Ⓒ Include what the actors wore too
Ⓓ Describe the color of the dresses

1`. t has a value of $\frac{5}{2}$. p is the sum of t and v, and p has a value of 0. What is the value of v?

  Ⓐ $\frac{-1}{3}$

  Ⓑ 4

  Ⓒ 2.5

  Ⓓ $\frac{-5}{2}$

2. What is the sum of 10 and −10?

  Ⓐ 20

  Ⓑ 0

  Ⓒ 1

  Ⓓ −20

3. If the value of r is $\frac{-1}{3}$ and t has a value of $\frac{-1}{2}$, will t + r be to the right or left of t on a number line, and why?

  Ⓐ To the left because the absolute value of r is less than the absolute value of t.
  Ⓑ To the right because the absolute value of r is less than the absolute value of t, and both numbers are negative.
  Ⓒ To the left because r is a negative value being added to t.
  Ⓓ To the left because the sum of two negative numbers is always negative.

4. Solve $\frac{9}{14}$ - $\frac{3}{14}$ and indicate it by shading the relevant boxes.

5. A person who is antisocial would NOT enjoy...

Ⓐ going to a big party.
Ⓑ spending time alone in his or her room.
Ⓒ playing video games.
Ⓓ hiking by him or herself.

6. Determine the meaning of the word digress based on the following affixes.

di-= to the opposite
gress=to go

Ⓐ the opposite of going
Ⓑ move away from the main topic
Ⓒ go on vacation
Ⓓ opposed to something

7. Based on your understanding of prefixes, when can you infer that something that is postmortem occurs?

The word postmortem is made up of two affixes:
post- + mortem
mortem means "life"

Ⓐ Before someone is born
Ⓑ During someone's life
Ⓒ After someone is dead
Ⓓ When someone is living

8. Based on the prefix, unacceptable means?

Ⓐ Sick
Ⓑ Bad
Ⓒ Good
Ⓓ Angry

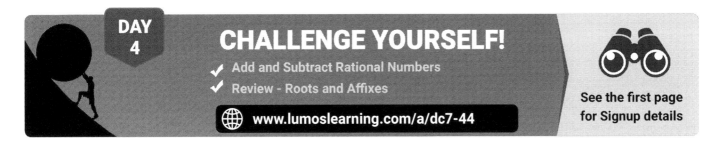

DAY 4

CHALLENGE YOURSELF!
✔ Add and Subtract Rational Numbers
✔ Review - Roots and Affixes

🌐 www.lumoslearning.com/a/dc7-44

See the first page
for Signup details

1. Greg is able to run a mile in 8 minutes. He ran at that pace for t minutes. What does the following expression represent?

$$\frac{t}{8}$$

- Ⓐ The number of miles that Greg ran.
- Ⓑ The number of hours that Greg ran.
- Ⓒ The average pace at which Greg ran.
- Ⓓ The amount of time it took Greg to run 8 miles.

2. What value could x NOT be in the following expression?:

$$\frac{5+x}{x}$$

- Ⓐ 5
- Ⓑ 1
- Ⓒ −5
- Ⓓ 0

3. Rose is filling her swimming pool with water. She needs to pump 2000 gallons into the pool, and the water flows at a rate of r gallons per hour. Which of the following expresses the amount of time it will take to fill the pool?

- Ⓐ $\dfrac{2000}{r}$
- Ⓑ 2000r
- Ⓒ 2000 + r
- Ⓓ $\dfrac{r}{2000}$

4. Complete the fraction: $\dfrac{?}{3} = -5$. Write your answer in the box given below.

While reading his science textbook, Jorge comes across the following sentence: Animals are part of different ecosystems around the world.

When Jorge finds the word "ecosystem" in the dictionary he sees the following:

Ecosystem n. (ek-o-sys-tem)
1. a community of interacting organisms
2. a general term to describe a complex system

5. What do the letters in parentheses represent?

     Ⓐ The word's part of speech
     Ⓑ How to pronounce the word
     Ⓒ The main meaning of the word
     Ⓓ The secondary meaning of the word

While reading his science textbook, Jorge comes across the following sentence: Animals are part of different ecosystems around the world.

When Jorge finds the word "ecosystem" in the dictionary he sees the following:

Ecosystem n. (ek-o-sys-tem)
1. a community of interacting organisms
2. a general term to describe a complex system

6. Based on the dictionary entry, what part of speech is the word "ecosystem"?

     Ⓐ Adjective
     Ⓑ Noun
     Ⓒ Pronoun
     Ⓓ Verb

While reading his science textbook, Jorge comes across the following sentence: Animals are part of different ecosystems around the world.

When Jorge finds the word "ecosystem" in the dictionary he sees the following:

Ecosystem n. (ek-o-sys-tem)
1. a community of interacting organisms
2. a general term to describe a complex system

7. Which definition best fits the word "ecosystem" in the sentence Jorge read?

     Ⓐ A community of interacting organisms
     Ⓑ A general term used to describe a complex system

Lynn is looking for a synonym to use in her essay, so she opens the thesaurus. She looks up the following entry.

delay v. 1. Storms delayed the construction process. curb, detain, hamper, hinder, hold. 2. He delayed his admission until he got back from Europe. postpone, hold, put off, shelve. 3. Don't delay, the sale is almost over. hedge, hang back, hesitate, pause, stall.

8. Lynn wants to write a piece that encourages students to express the concerns to the principal without causing her to delay. Which would be the BEST synonym to use in her piece? Circle the correct answer choice.

 Ⓐ Hesitate
 Ⓑ Put off
 Ⓒ Hinder
 Ⓓ Shelve

THIS WEEK'S ONLINE ACTIVITIES

✔ Reading Assignment   ✔ Vocabulary Practice
✔ Write Your Summer Diary

 www.lumoslearning.com/a/slh7-8

See the first page
for Signup details

WEEKLY FUN SUMMER PHOTO CONTEST

📷 Take a picture of your summer fun activity and share it on Twitter or Instagram

Use the #SummerLearning mention

@LumosLearning on	@lumos.learning on
🐦	📷
Twitter	**Instagram**

Tag friends and increase your chances of winning the contest.

PARTICIPATE AND STAND A CHANCE TO WIN $50 AMAZON GIFT CARD!

WEEK 10
LUMOS SHORT STORY COMPETITION 2023

Write a short story based on your summer experiences and get a chance to win **$100 cash prize + 1 year free subscription to Lumos StepUp + trophy with a certificate**.

To enter the competition follow the instructions.

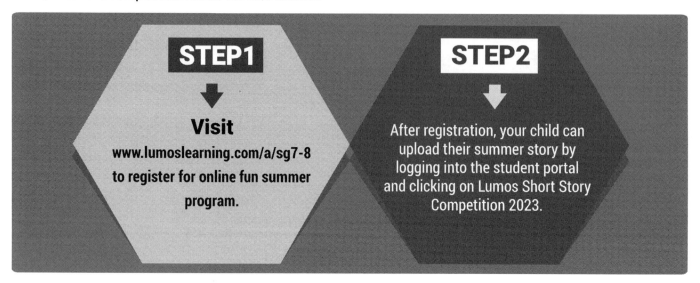

STEP1

Visit
www.lumoslearning.com/a/sg7-8
to register for online fun summer
program.

STEP2

After registration, your child can upload their summer story by logging into the student portal and clicking on Lumos Short Story Competition 2023.

Note: If you have already registered this book and are using online resources, you need not register again. Students can simply log in to the student portal and submit their story for the competition.

Visit: **www.lumoslearning.com/a/slh2023** for more information

Last date for submission is August 31, 2023

Use the space provided below for scratch work before uploading your summer story Scratch Work

"Two years ago, my world turned upside down. Everything shut down, and by the time summer hit, all hopes of a normal summer were eradicated. This summer, however, was a big step up from the summers of 2020 and 2021. This summer, Covid still affected our lives with mask wearing, social distancing, and limited activities but it was a step towards normalcy. Though Covid is still prominent, my family and I eased our way out of our previously covid monopolized summers.

The first big step towards normalcy this summer was when my sister and I rejoined my local track team.It felt strange to be back and running in a sports mask, but it also felt good, normal. Training with my team and reconnecting after two years of leave was challenging. Many old families left and many new families joined. I had to make new friends and work very hard to return to championship competition shape. By the end of the season, I mostly regained what I lost , and I even got to compete in the AAU Jr. Olympics along with my sister! Though this years track season was different, it was definitely a step in a positive direction.

The next step my family and I took to a normal summer was restarting our family day trips. We went to farms for fresh fruit picking, to a museum for fun and learning, and to a zoo and aquarium as well. This summer was also my first time back to a restaurant since 2020. We still had to wear masks and only removed them when we were actively eating; it was a new way of dining, but I still enjoyed the experience with my family.

Though my family and I did much more outside our house this year. We still enjoyed each others company at home. For example, on Independence Day we threw water balloons, played in our pool, ate my dad's BBQ, and popped fireworks at home. My sister and I also continued to craft and make cool artwork. My siblings also did homemade science experiments with our science kits. We also continued our family bike riding, movie nights, and camping and making smores in our backyard.

Even though this summer was not completely normal and covid free, I still enjoyed it. I wouldnt trade this summer for anything because this summer will be a happy, special, and memorable summer in which I will forever share with my family.

Student Name: Abi Pear
Grade: 8

2021 Winning Story

In March 2020, I found out that my 7th-grade exams were canceled. At first, I was excited, but I soon realized that these changes would upend my expectations for school. Over time, my classmates and I realized that the global coronavirus pandemic was not something to be excited about and would have long-lasting effects on our education. My school canceled exams again this year, and, strangely, I found myself missing them. The virus has revealed global inequality regarding health.

Even as America fights the virus, so is it also fighting racism and injustice. The Black Lives Matter movement has shown me how brutal racism can be. The deaths of George Floyd and Breonna Taylor, two African Americans killed by police for no reason, have made me aware of the dangerous injustice in America. Hatred and violence against Asian immigrants are also on the rise. People of color in the US are routinely subjected to prejudice, if not also violence, at the hands of white people. Chinese people are blamed for the "China virus,"; which has led to Asian Americans being attacked. Enduring forms of racism are preventing progress around the world. Racism in society takes many forms, including prejudice, discrimination, and microaggressions. If racism is systemic in America, there will never be true peace or equality until it is uprooted. People see me as a person of color and assume that I'm from Africa because of the color of my skin, even though I am half Black and half white. I don't seem to earn as much respect as a white person would because I am thought of as a foreigner, not a true American. It makes me feel unwelcome and unwanted. I am lucky to have access to technology to keep me engaged in learning. There are still others who don't have the ability to continue learning, whose educational institutions have been shut down by the virus. I have learned that so many people lack access to basic necessities and that racism in America continues to lead to violence and injustice. I aspire to work toward a system that addresses these inequalities in the future. This summer I reflected back on all these things and have learned that no matter what, we all should continue to push on, even through hardships and obstacles.

Student Name: Nora Moor
Grade: 8

PREVENT SUMMER LEARNING LOSS WITH 7 SIMPLE STEPS

Summer Learning loss is defined as "a loss of knowledge and skills . . . most commonly due to . . . . extended breaks [during the summertime]" (from edglossary.org/learning-loss). Many teachers have certainly had the experience of taking the first month of school not only to introduce his or her rules and procedures to the class but also to get the kids back "up to speed" with thinking, remembering what they've learned . . . and in many cases, reviewing previous content. With a traditional school calendar, then, this can mean that up to 10% of the school year is spent playing catch-up.

What's a parent to do? Fortunately, there are some simple steps you can take with your child to help your son or daughter both enjoy the summer and keep those all-important skills honed and fresh:

(1) Read!

Research supports the relationship between independent reading and student achievement, so simply having your child read daily will make a positive difference. Check out the following sources to find books that your child will want to dive into: your public library, local bookstores, online stores (Amazon, Barnes and Noble, half.com, etc.), and yard sales (if the family hosting the sale has children a bit older than your own, you stand a good chance of scoring discarded books that are a perfect match for your son or daughter's reading level).

(2) Write!

Have your child write letters to out-of-town friends and family, or write postcards while on vacation. A summer journal is another way to document summer activities. For the artistic or tech-savvy child, you may choose to create a family scrapbook with captions (consider the online options at Shutterfly, Mixbook, and Smilebox). Not only will you preserve this summer's memories, but your child will also continue to practice his or her writing skills! (See Summer is Here! Ideas to Keep Your Child's Writing Skills Sharp for more writing ideas.)

(3) Do the Math!

Think of ways your child can incorporate math skills into daily activities: have a yard sale, and put your child in charge of the cash box; help younger ones organize a lemonade stand (to practice salesmanship and making change). Or simply purchase a set of inexpensive flash cards to practice basic facts while waiting in line or on a long car ride. There's even a host of free online games that will keep your child's math skills sharp.

(4) "Homeschool" Your Child

Keeping your child's skills fresh doesn't have to cost a fortune: check out some of the Lumos Learning workbooks and online resources (at lumoslearning.com/store), and your child can work through several exercises each day. Even as little as twenty minutes a day can yield positive results, and it's easy to work in a small block of time here and there. For instance, your child can work in the book during a car ride, right before bedtime, etc. Or, simply make this part of your child's morning routine. For example: wake up, eat breakfast, complete chores, and then work in the workbook for 20 minutes. With time, you can make this a natural habit.

(5) Go Back-to-School Shopping (For a Great Summer School Learning Experience)

Check out offerings from the big names (think Sylvan, Huntington, Mathnasium, and Kumon), and also consider local summer schools. Some school districts and local colleges provide learning programs: research the offerings on-line for more information regarding the available options in your area.

(6) Take a Hike . . . Go Camping!

But "camp" doesn't always involve pitching a tent in the great outdoors. Nowadays, there are camps for every interest: sports camps, art camp, music camp, science camp, writing camp . . . the possibilities are endless! With a quick Internet search, you'll be able to turn up multiple options that will appeal to your son or daughter. And even if these camps aren't "academic", the life skills and interpersonal experiences are certain to help your child succeed in the "real world". For example, working together as a cast to put on a summer theater production involves memorizing lines, cooperation, stage crew coordination, and commitment – all skills that can come in handy when it comes to fostering a good work ethic and the ability to collaborate with others.

(7) Get tutored

Many teachers offer tutoring services throughout the summer months, either for individuals or small groups of students. Even the most school-averse student tends to enjoy the personal attention of a former teacher in a setting outside of the classroom. Plus, a tutor can tailor his or her instruction to pinpoint your child's needs – so you can maximize the tutoring sessions with the skills and concepts your child needs the most help with.

Of course, you don't need to do all seven steps to ensure that your child maintains his or her skills. Just following through with one or two of these options will go a long way toward continued learning, skills maintenance, and easing the transition to school when summer draws to a close.

As mentioned in our "Beating Summer Academic Loss" article, students are at risk of losing academic ground during the summer months, especially with respect to their reading level, spelling, and vocabulary. One of the best ways to prevent this "brain drain" for literacy is to have your son or daughter read each day during the summer break.

Better yet, you can promote these all-important skills and participate in your child's summer reading by engaging in active dialogue with your son or daughter. Below are several questions and ideas for discussion that will promote comprehension, recall, and critical thinking skills. In addition, these questions reflect several of the Common Core standards – which underpin the curriculum, instruction and standardized testing for most school districts. Of course, the standards vary by grade level, but some of the common themes that emerge in these standards are: citing evidence, summarizing, and making inferences.

• Citing evidence

Simply put, citing evidence involves going back into the text (book, magazine, newspaper, etc.) and finding "proof" to back up an answer, opinion, or assertion. For instance, you could ask your child, "Did you enjoy this book?" and then follow up that "yes" or "no" response with a "Why?" This requires the reader to provide details and examples from the story to support his or her opinion. For this particular question, then, your child may highlight plot events he or she liked, character attributes, writing style, and even genre (type of book) as evidence. Challenge for older students: Ask your child to go back into the text and find a direct quote to support an opinion or answer.

• **Summarizing**

For nonfiction pieces, this may involve being able to explain the 5W's – who, what, where, when, why (and how). For literature, ask your child to summarize the story elements, including: the setting, characters, main conflict or problem, events, resolution, and theme/lesson/moral. If your child can do this with specificity and accuracy, there's a very good chance that he or she comprehended the story. Challenge for older students: Ask your child to identify more complex story elements, such as the climax, rising action, and falling action.

• **Making inferences**

Making an inference is commonly referred to as "reading between the lines." That is, the reader can't find the answer to a question directly in the text but instead must synthesize or analyze information to come to a conclusion. To enhance these higher-level thinking skills, ask your child to describe the main character's personality, describe how a character changed by the end of a novel, or detail how the setting influenced the story's plot. Challenge for older students: Have the reader compare and contrast two or more characters to highlight similarities and differences in personality, actions, etc.

Of course, if you read the same book that your child reads, you'll be able to come up with even more detailed questions – and also know if your child truly understood the reading based on his or her answers! But even if you don't get a chance to read what your child does, simply asking some of these questions not only helps your child's reading skills but also demonstrates an interest in your child – and his or her reading.

BEATING THE BRAIN DRAIN THROUGH LITERACY WEBINAR RECAP WITH PRINTABLE ACTIVITY SHEET

Lumos Learning conducted webinar on "Beating the Brain Drain Through Literacy." During this webinar, we provided the students with several ideas for keeping their literacy skills sharp in the summertime.

Here's a handy chart with the ideas from the webinar, ready for you to post on your refrigerator. Let your child pick and choose the activities that appeal to him or her. Of course, reading should be nonnegotiable, but the list below provides alternatives for reluctant readers – or for those who just don't enjoy reading a traditional fiction novel. The first set of activities touch upon ideas that reinforce writing skills, while the second half addresses reading skills. There is also room on the chart to date or check off activities your child has completed.

Skill Area	Activity	Completion date	Notes for parents
Writing skills, spelling, and/or vocabulary	Keep a journal (things you do, places you go, people you meet)		Even though journals work on spelling skills, be sure your child understands that spelling "doesn't count". Most children like to keep their journals private, so they don't need to worry about perfect skills or that someone else is going to read/grade what they wrote.
	Start a blog		Enable privacy settings to keep viewers limited to friends and family. Check out WordPress, Squarespace, and Quillpad to begin blogging.
	Get published		The following places publish student work: The Clairmont Review, CyberKids, Creative Kids Magazine, New Moon, and The Young Writer's Magazine.
	Write letters		Have your child write or type letters, postcards, and emails to friends and family members.

	Take part in a family movie night		Watch movies that are thought-provoking to elicit interesting post-movie discussions. Other good bets are movies that are based on a book (read the book first and compare the two).
	Organize a family game night		Choose word games to work on spelling and vocabulary skills (examples: Scrabble, Boggle, and Hangman).
Reading skills: fluency, comprehension, critical thinking, decoding skills,inferencing, etc.	Pick up a good book!		Places to find/buy/borrow books include: your public library, ebooks, yard sales, book stores, your child's school library (if it's open during the summer), and borrowed books from friends and family members.
	Read materials that aren't "books"...		Ideas include: karaoke lyrics, cereal boxes, newspapers, magazines for kids, billboards, close captioning, and audio books.
	Compete! Enter a reading challenge		Scholastic Reading hosts a competition called "Reading Under the Stars" to break a world record for minutes read. Barnes and Noble gives students the opportunity to earn one free book with "Imagination's Destination" reading challenge.

Note: Reading just six books over the summer can maintain – and sometimes even increase! – your child's reading level. Not sure if the book is appropriate for your child's reading level? Use the five-finger rule: have your son/daughter read a page of a book. Each time your child encounters a word that is unfamiliar or unknown, he or she holds up a finger. If your child holds up more than five fingers on a given page, that book is probably too difficult.

However, there are some books that a child will successfully tackle if it's high-interest to him or her. Keep in mind that reading levels are a guide (as is the five-finger rule), and some children may exceed expectations...so don't hold your child back if he or she really wants to read a particular book (even if it may appear to be too challenging).

Remember, if students do some of these simple activities, they can prevent the typical four to six weeks of learning loss due to the "summer slide." And since spelling, vocabulary and reading skills are vulnerable areas, be sure to encourage your child to maintain his or her current literacy level...it will go a long way come September!

SUMMER IS HERE! KEEP YOUR CHILD'S WRITING SKILLS SHARP WITH ONLINE GAMES

Like Reading and math, free online activities exist for all subjects... and writing is no exception. Check out the following free interactive writing activities, puzzles, quizzes and games that reinforce writing skills and encourage creativity:

Primary Level (K-2nd Grade)

Story Writing Game

In this game, the child fills in the blanks of a short story. The challenge is for the storyteller to choose words that fit the kind of story that has been selected. For example, if the child chooses to tell a ghost story, then he or she must select words for each blank that would be appropriate for a scary tale.
http://www.funenglishgames.com/writinggames/story.html

Opinions Quiz for Critical Thinking

Practice developing logical reasons to support a thesis with this interactive activity. Students read the stated opinion, such as, "We should have longer recess because..." The child must then select all of the possible reasons from a list that would support the given statement. The challenge lies with the fact that each statement may have more than one possible answer, and to receive credit, the student must select all correct responses. This game is best suited for older primary students.
http://www.netrover.com/~kingskid/Opinion/opinion.html

Interactives: Sequence

Allow your child to practice ordering events with this interactive version of the fairy tale, Cinderella. The child looks at several pictures from the story and must drag them to the bottom of the screen to put the events in chronological order. When the player mouses over each scene from the story, a sentence describing the image appears and is read aloud to the student. Once the events are in order, the student can learn more about the plot and other story elements with the accompanying tutorials and lessons.
http://www.learner.org/interactives/story/sequence.html

BEATING SUMMER ACADEMIC LOSS
AN INFORMATIVE GUIDE TO PARENTS

The "Summer Slide"

First, it's important to understand the implications of "summer slide" – otherwise known as summer learning loss. Research has shown that some students who take standardized tests in the fall could have lost up to 4-6 weeks of learning each school year (when compared with test results from the previous spring). This means that teachers end up dedicating the first month of each new school year for reviewing material before they can move onto any new content and concepts.

The three areas that suffer most from summer learning loss are in the areas of vocabulary/reading, spelling, and math. In Stop! In the Name of Education: Prevent Summer Learning Loss With 7 Simple Steps, we discussed some activities parents could use with children to prevent summer slide. Let's add to that list with even more ways to keep children engaged and learning – all summer long.

Be sure to check out:

•Your Child's School

Talk to child's teacher, and tell him or her that you'd like to work on your child's academics over the summer. Most teachers will have many suggestions for you.

In addition to the classroom teacher as a resource, talk to the front office staff and guidance counselors. Reading lists and summer programs that are organized through the school district may be available for your family, and these staff members can usually point you in the right direction.

•Your Community

A quick Google search for "free activities for kids in (insert your town's name)" will yield results of possible educational experiences and opportunities in your area. Some towns offer "dollar days", park lunches, and local arts and entertainment.

You may even wish to involve your child in the research process to find fun, affordable memberships and discounts to use at area attractions. For New Jerseyans and Coloradans, check out www.funnewjersey.com and www.colorado.com for ideas.

Of course, don't forget your local library! In addition to books, you can borrow movies and audiobooks, check out the latest issue of your favorite magazine, and get free Internet access on the library's computers. Most libraries offer a plethora of other educational choices, too – from book clubs and author visits to movie nights and crafts classes, you're sure to find something at your local branch that your child will enjoy.

•Stores

This is an extremely engaging activity – and your child won't even know he or she is learning! For grocery shopping, ask your child to write the list while you dictate. At the store, your son/daughter can locate the items and keep a cost tally to stay within a specified budget. At the checkout, you can have a contest to see whose estimate of the final bill is most accurate – and then reward the winner!

You may wish to plan a home improvement project or plant a garden: for this, your child can make the list, research the necessary materials, and then plan and execute the project after a visit to your local home improvement store. All of these activities involve those three critical areas of spelling, vocabulary/reading, and math.

•The Kitchen

This is one of the best places to try new things – by researching new foods, recipes, and discussing healthy food choices – while practicing math skills (such as measuring ingredients, doubling recipes, etc.). Your child may also enjoy reading about new cultures and ethnicities and then trying out some new menu items from those cultures.

•The Television

TV doesn't have to be mind numbing … when used appropriately. You can watch sports with your child to review stats and make predictions; watch documentaries; or tune into the History Channel, Discovery, National Geographic, HGTV, and more. Anything that teaches, helps your child discover new interests, and promotes learning new things together is fair game.

As an extension, you may decide to research whether or not the show portrays accurate information. And for those children who really get "into" a certain topic, you can enrich their learning by taking related trips to the museum, doing Internet research, and checking out books from the library that tie into the topic of interest.

•Movies

Movies can be educational, too, if you debrief with your child afterwards. Schedule a family movie night, and then discuss how realistic the movie was, what the messages were, etc.

For book-based movies (such as Judy Moody, Harry Potter, Percy Jackson, etc.), you could read the book together first, and then view the movie version. Comparing and contrasting the two is another terrific educational way to enjoy time together and work on your child's reasoning skills.

Note: www.imdb.com and www.commonsensemedia.org are great sites for movie recommendations and movie reviews for kids and families.

•Games

Playing games promotes taking turns, reading and math skills, and strategy development. Scour yard sales for affordable board games like Scrabble, Monopoly, Uno, Battleship, and Qwirkle.

Don't forget about non-board games, like those found on the Wii, Nintendo, Xbox, and other gaming consoles. You'll still want to choose wisely and limit your child's screen time, but these electronic versions of popular (and new) games mirror the way kids think ... while focusing on reading and math skills. For more ideas, Google "education apps" for suggestions.

·Books, books, books!

Of course, nothing beats reading for maintaining skills. When you can connect your child with a book that is of interest to him or her, it can be fun for your child, build confidence, and improve fluency.

To help your child find a book that's "just right", use the five-finger rule: choose a page from a possible book and have your child read that page. Every time he or she encounters an unknown word, put up a finger. If your child exceeds five fingers (that is, five unknown words), that book is probably too challenging and he or she may wish to pass on it.

For reluctant readers, consider non-book reading options, like:magazines (such as Ranger Rick, American Girl, Discovery Kids, and Sports Illustrated for Kids), cereal boxes, billboards, current events, closed captioning, and karaoke. If you keep your eyes open, you'll find there are many natural reading opportunities that surround us every day.

Whatever you do, remember to keep it fun. Summer is a time for rest and rejuvenation, and learning doesn't always have to be scheduled. In fact, some of the most educational experiences are unplanned.

Visit lumoslearning.com/parents/summer-program for more information.

VALUABLE LEARNING EXPERIENCES
A SUMMER ACTIVITY GUIDE FOR PARENTS

Soon school will be out of session, leaving the summer free for adventure and relaxation. However, it's important to also use the summer for learning activities. Giving your son or daughter opportunities to keep learning can result in more maturity, self-growth, curiosity, and intelligence. Read on to learn some ways to make the most of this summer.

Read

Summer is the perfect time to get some extra reading accomplished. Youth can explore books about history, art, animals, and other interests, or they can read classic novels that have influenced people for decades. A lot of libraries have summer fun reading programs which give children, teens, and adults little weekly prizes for reading books. You can also offer a reward, like a $25 gift card, if your child reads a certain amount of books.

Travel

"The World is a book and those who do not travel read only a page." This quote by Saint Augustine illustrates why travel is so important for a student (and even you!). Travel opens our eyes to new cultures, experiences, and challenges. When you travel, you see commonalities and differences between cultures.

Professor Adam Galinsky of Columbia Business School, who has researched travel benefits, said in a Quartz article that travel can help a child develop compassion and empathy: "Engaging with another culture helps kids recognize that their own egocentric way of looking at the world is not the only way of being in the world."

If the student in your life constantly complains about not having the newest iPhone, how would they feel seeing a child in a third-world country with few possessions? If you child is disrespectful and self-centered, what would they learn going to Japan and seeing a culture that promotes respect and otherness instead of self-centeredness?

If you can't afford to travel to another country, start a family travel fund everyone can contribute to and in the meantime, travel somewhere new locally! Many people stay in the area they live instead of exploring. Research attractions in your state and nearby states to plan a short road trip to fun and educational places!

Visit Museums

You can always take your children to visit museums. Spending some quality time at a museum can enhance curiosity because children can learn new things, explore their interests, or see exhibits expanding upon school subjects they recently studied. Many museums have seasonal exhibits, so research special exhibits nearby. For example, "Titanic: The Artifact Exhibition" has been making its way to various museums in the United States. It contains items recovered from the Titanic as well as interactive activities and displays explaining the doomed ship's history and tragic demise. This year, the exhibit is visiting Las Vegas, Orlando, and Waco.

Work

A final learning suggestion for the summer is for students to get a job, internship, or volunteer position. Such jobs can help with exploring career options. For example, if your child is thinking of becoming a vet, they could walk dogs for neighbors, or if your child wants to start their own business, summer is the perfect time to make and sell products.

Not only will a job or volunteer work look good on college applications, but it will also teach your children valuable life lessons that can result in more maturity and responsibility. You could enhance the experience by teaching them accounting and illustrating real world problems to them, like budgeting money for savings and bills.

The above suggestions are just four of the many ways you can help learning continue for your child or children all summer long. Experience and seeing things first-hand are some of the most important ways that students can learn, so we hope you find the above suggestions helpful in designing a fun, educational, and rewarding summer that will have benefits in and out of the classroom.

NOTES

What if I buy more than one Lumos Study Program?

Step 1 ⟶ **Visit the URL given below and login to your parent account**

www.lumoslearning.com

Step 2 ⟶ Click on the horizontal lines (≡) in the top right-hand corner of the parent account and select **"My tedBooks"**

Place the Book Access Code and submit (See the first page for access code).

Step 3 ⟶ **Add the new book**

To add the new book for a registered student, choose the **'Student'** button and click on submit.

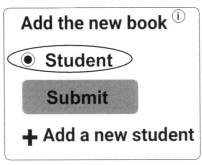

To add the new book for a new student, choose the **'Add New Student'** button and complete the student registration.

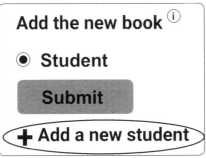

Lumos tedBooks for State Test Practice

Lumos tedBook for standardized test practice provides necessary grade-specific state assessment practice and skills mastery. Each tedBook includes hundreds of standards-aligned practice questions and online summative assessments that mirror actual state tests.

The workbook provides students access to thousands of valuable learning resources such as worksheets, videos, apps, books, and much more.

Lumos Learning tedBooks for State Assessment	
SBAC Math & ELA Practice Book	CA, CT, DE, HI, ID, ME, MI, MN, NV, ND, OR, WA, WI
NJSLA Math & ELA Practice Book	NJ
ACT Aspire Math & ELA Practice Book	AL, AR
IAR Math & ELA Practice Book	IL
FSA Math & ELA Practice Book	FL
PARCC Math & ELA Practice Book	DC, NM
GMAS Math & ELA Practice Book	GA
NYST Math & ELA Practice Book	NY
ILEARN Math & ELA Practice Book	IN
LEAP Math & ELA Practice Book	LA
MAP Math & ELA Practice Book	MO
MAAP Math & ELA Practice Book	MS
AASA Math & ELA Practice Book	AZ
MCAP Math & ELA Practice Book	MD
OST Math & ELA Practice Book	OH
MCAS Math & ELA Practice Book	MA
CMAS Math & ELA Practice Book	CO
TNReady Math & ELA Practice Book	TN
STAAR Math & ELA Practice Book	TX
NM-MSSA Math & ELA Practice Book	NM

Available

- At Leading book stores
- www.lumoslearning.com/a/lumostedbooks

Made in the USA
Middletown, DE
02 July 2023

34004152R00121